Thomas Aquinas

Saints by Our Side

Thomas Aquinas

By Marianne Lorraine Trouvé, FSP

Pauline

BOOKS & MEDIA

Boston

Library of Congress Cataloging-in-Publication Data

Names: Trouvé, Marianne Lorraine, author.
Title: Thomas Aquinas / by Marianne Lorraine Trouv?e, FSP.
Description: Boston, MA : Pauline Books & Media, 2018. | Series: Saints by our side |
Includes bibliographical references.
Identifiers: LCCN 2017038169| ISBN 9780819875402 (pbk.) | ISBN 0819875406
(pbk.)
Subjects: LCSH: Thomas, Aquinas, Saint, 1225?-1274.
Classification: LCC BX4700.T6 T765 2018 | DDC 230/.2092 [B] --dc23
LC record available at https://lccn.loc.gov/2017038169

The Scripture quotations contained herein are from the *New Revised Standard Version Bible: Catholic Edition,* copyright © 1989, 1993, Division of Christian Education of the National Council of the Churches of Christ in the United States of America. Used by permission. All rights reserved.

Excerpts from papal and magisterium texts copyright © Libreria Editrice Vaticana. Used with permission.

Every effort has been made to trace copyright holders and to obtain their permission for the use of copyrighted material. The publisher apologizes if there are any errors or omissions in the above list. If any permissions have been inadvertently overlooked, the publisher will be pleased to make the necessary and reasonable arrangements at the first opportunity.

Cover design by Rosana Usselmann

Cover art: Bartolomé Esteban Murillo, courtesy of Wikimedia Commons; background image: istockphoto.com/© Plateresca

"P" and PAULINE are registered trademarks of the Daughters of St. Paul.

Published by Pauline Books & Media, 50 Saint Pauls Avenue, Boston, MA 02130-3491

Printed in the U.S.A.

www.pauline.org

Pauline Books & Media is the publishing house of the Daughters of St. Paul, an international congregation of women religious serving the Church with the communications media.

1 2 3 4 5 6 7 8 9   22 21 20 19 18

Contents

Can a Medieval Friar
Capture Your Heart?

The Aquino family castle still sits atop a craggy hill in Roccasecca, Italy. Small grassy plants cover the rocks on the slope of the hill. On a clear day, a few wispy clouds might float through the deep blue sky, but one can still see the valley below and, looking toward Rome, the hills in the north.

Medieval castles can conjure up images of dashing knights seeking to find and rescue their beautiful ladies-in-waiting. And in a sense, Saint Thomas Aquinas was a knight, but not the Don Quixote type who jousts with windmills. Thomas was a knight in search of the truth, always seeking his lady: Wisdom. This text from the Book of Wisdom could describe him: "I prayed, and understanding was given me; I called on God, and the spirit of wisdom came to me. I preferred her to scepters and thrones, and I accounted wealth as nothing in comparison with her" (7:7–8). Some of his spiritual knight-errantry included running away from home to follow his dream and stubbornly persisting in it even when his family kidnapped him. They held him under house arrest for a year but Thomas didn't waver. Some years later, at the University of Paris, he walked through crowds of rioting students in order to get to his classroom to teach, despite the sticks and stones flying through the air. This knight did not wear shining armor and carried no sword. Instead, he put the belt of truth around his waist, wore the helmet of salvation, and carried the sword of the Spirit, which is the word of God (see Eph 6:14–17). Thomas sought truth in God. The word of God became his constant companion and the light of his life.

A Friend of Truth

Once I was at a talk in which the speaker mentioned Thomas in reference to a theological point. Then he said that while he has a great respect for Thomas, he didn't consider him to be like a friend. Immediately I thought, "Oh no, that's not the way it is for me. Thomas is my *friend!* I love him."

The Book of Wisdom continues, "In every generation [Wisdom] passes into holy souls and makes them friends of God, and prophets" (7:27). In his generation Thomas Aquinas was one of the foremost friends of wisdom, and so he became a prophet—not a prophet in the sense of predicting the future, but of speaking the word of God. For that is the primary task of a prophet. As a friend of God and now a saint in heaven, Thomas can be our friend too. Like all the saints, he is ready to intercede for our needs.

As a child I was rather quiet and shy, drawn to books. I loved spending time in the library and in the summer would try to read as many books as I could. The first time I heard about Thomas at my Catholic grammar school, I thought, "A saint who loves books? He's my kind of saint!" I read Louis de Wohl's novel about Thomas, *The Quiet Light.* I asked my older brother Paul, who was in high school and liked to read about the saints, to tell me all he knew about Saint Thomas. Two things stood out: Thomas was quiet, and he read and wrote books. I could identify with both of those, and in effect it was love at first sight. Gradually, over time, as I read more about Thomas and even started to ask his intercession, I felt him to be more and more of a friend. He captured my heart.

Thomas was enigmatic, though, and that added to his mystique. Other great saints, such as Augustine, wrote freely of their own struggles and desires along the way of holiness. Augustine's passion and penetrating analysis of his inner life in *The Confessions* can easily resonate with people in its pathos and depth. But Thomas did not write about himself. He wrote thousands of pages, but nothing about his personal life, although here and there he does drop a few clues. For example, in discussing the role that memory plays in the virtue of prudence, he offers four tips to cultivate a good memory (see *Summa Theol.,* II-II, q. 49, a. 1). I suspect that Thomas used those aids in developing his own prodigious memory. But even such slightly revealing texts are rare in his writings. Yet the lack of personal information can also tell us something about him. It probably reflects his personality as a studious, reflective person. The scholarly texts that he wrote didn't lend themselves to personal disclosure. His sole aim was to write for the glory of God and to fulfill his mission as a Dominican friar, which was to preach. Thomas exhausted himself in writing commentaries on the Bible and on the works of Aristotle in order to help the young Dominican friars in their studies. His motive for doing all this work was not to glorify himself but to help others. He became a saint because of his humility and love.

His humility is all the more striking because Thomas was certainly one of the great geniuses of Western thought. Though he is best known for his *Summa Theologiae* and *Summa Contra Gentiles,* his writings run to about fifty large folio volumes containing over eight million words[1] in thousands of pages. Thomas played a key role in helping the Church to use the thought of the philosopher Aristotle, which was then becoming better known in the West. Though controversial at the time, especially at the University of Paris where Thomas taught, he always discussed Aristotle's teachings in the clear light of reason and faith. He never stooped to personal attacks, but dealt with the issues. That in itself is a great lesson for us today, when it's so easy, especially online, to shoot down other people or quickly send out anonymous zingers. Thomas is a model of charity and civility in discourse. Instead of criticizing people, he critiqued ideas.

About twenty-five years ago I decided to read the *Summa*. I thought that if I read an article a day, I could finish it in about seven years. I still haven't finished it! But that's all right because it's more important to read Thomas slowly and savor his writing like a fine Italian wine. Reading Thomas is both challenging and engaging. Sometimes I struggle to get his meaning, and at other times he leaves me in awe at a profound yet beautifully simple response. I love his logic, how he sets out his points one by one, puts objections up front, and responds to each one. I was particularly drawn to how he describes grace, especially how Jesus gives us grace and works through the sacraments. I also liked his idea that charity or love is friendship with God.[2] Thomas has become a great guide for my spiritual life. The ideas he presents in the *Summa* are not just abstract theological points, but profound spiritual wisdom on how to live a holy life.

Perhaps because he grew up in the sunny Italian countryside, Thomas seems to have had a happy disposition. He had an optimistic view of human life and its possibilities. While he certainly observed the rules of his Dominican order, he was not known for doing extreme penances. Instead, doing what God asked of him each day was his way to holiness, something that we can do too. Thomas had a deep understanding of human nature and sympathy for its weaknesses. For example, in discussing how much time we should spend in prayer, he noted that we have our limits, writing, "It is fitting that prayer should last long enough to kindle the fervor of interior desire, but when it exceeds this measure, so that it cannot be continued any longer without causing weariness, it should be discontinued" (*Summa Theol.,* II-II, q. 83, a. 14).

Thomas was a great friend of God, and ultimately that is why we honor him: it's what made him a saint. His philosophical and theological writings are enduring treasures, but if that's all we remember about Thomas, we are missing the secret of his greatness. Through the centuries he has touched countless people through his great Eucharistic hymns, drawing them into a deeper love for the Lord. How many times Catholics have gathered to worship Jesus present in the Eucharist at a Benediction service, and amid the fragrant clouds of incense they sing the words Thomas penned in his famous hymn *Tantum Ergo*:

> Down in adoration falling,
> Lo! the sacred Host we hail,
> Lo! o'er ancient forms departing
> Newer rites of grace prevail;
> Faith for all defects supplying,
> Where the feeble senses fail.

Perhaps by his silence about himself, Thomas wanted to point us to the One who really matters: Jesus Christ. A beautiful story that has come down to us captures the essence of Thomas' life. Once, after having written his great Eucharistic hymns, Thomas was praying on his knees before a crucifix. Suddenly the crucifix seemed to come to life and Thomas heard a voice saying, "You have written well of me, Thomas. What reward would you like?" He replied, "Only you, Lord, only you."[3]

Thomas had found the secret to happiness and holiness in his friendship with the Lord. And Thomas is ready to befriend us, too. I hope that everyone who reads this book will find in Thomas not only a great theologian and philosopher, but also a great friend: "Faithful friends are a sturdy shelter: whoever finds one has found a treasure" (Sir 6:14).

• • • • • • • • • • • •

CHAPTER ONE

A Determined Young Man

The Aquinas castle towered high into the sky in the sleepy little town of Roccasecca (dry rock) in Italy—a perfect setting for the birth of a giant. Thomas Aquinas was that giant, not only because he was a great philosopher and theologian, but because he was a saint. Like all the saints, however, he was not born a saint but had to struggle like we all do.

While the exact date of his birth is unknown, he was probably born in 1224 or 1225. Thomas came from a rather well-to-do family. Since the tenth century they had held lands in Roccasecca, located in what was then known as the Kingdom of the Two Sicilies. The town was about halfway between Rome and Naples. The family was known as "de Aquino" because in earlier years they had controlled the county of Aquino. Their location in Roccasecca was important because it placed them between the lands of the pope and the emperor.

Thomas was the son of Landolfo and Theodora. They had at least nine children, four boys and five girls. Thomas was the youngest of the boys. His two oldest brothers, Aimo and Rinaldo, were soldiers and fought in the army of the emperor, Frederick II. But they both switched sides and joined the papal forces when Frederick campaigned against the Pope. Of the third brother, Landolfo, we have no information.

Thomas' oldest sister, Marotta, became a Benedictine nun, while another sister, Theodora, married Count Roger of San Severino. The third, Maria, married William of San Severino, while a fourth, Adelasia, became the wife of Roger of Aquila. We don't know the name of the last girl, who died when she was a baby. Tragically, she was killed by lightning in a bad storm while she was sleeping in the castle. Thomas, then a toddler, was also taking a nap in the same room but was unharmed.[1] While we don't know all the details of this incident, it must have had a big effect on the little boy. His mother may have rushed in to the room, but perhaps in her grief would not have been able to comfort him. This incident may explain his lifelong fear of storms. Later, as a friar, on his frequent travels he would take with him a relic of Saint Agnes, whom he would invoke for protection during storms.

A legendary story about baby Thomas says that one day his mother and his nurse took him to the baths in Naples. Little Thomas picked up a piece of parchment from the ground and wouldn't let it go despite his nurse's prodding. Later, when his mother finally wrested it away from him, the paper was found to have the Hail Mary written on it. It's also said that whenever he would cry, he wouldn't stop unless someone gave him a parchment, which he would always put in his mouth. Naturally his early hagiographers made much of these stories, as if they indicated what he was destined to become. If they are true at all, it's more likely that baby Thomas just liked to put things in his mouth, as babies often do.

Life was good in the Aquinas castle. Perhaps Thomas acquired his generally optimistic view of things when he was a boy. He would have spent happy days playing with his brothers and sisters while his father oversaw the lands and his mother kept the household going. Mama Theodora was a very competent woman. As we will see from later events in Thomas' life, she helped her husband manage the family's affairs and did not shrink from asserting herself.

The Middle Ages were a time of faith, when people easily acknowledged God, and the Church played a large role in society. It was customary for the youngest son of noble families to be dedicated to the Church. The famous monastery of Monte Cassino was only about fifteen miles away from Roccasecca. Founded by Saint Benedict, it became one of the most important monastic centers in Europe. In Thomas' day, the monks ran a school for boys. His parents decided to send him there for his schooling, with the idea that he could later become a Benedictine monk. They probably assumed that with his family connections, he would eventually become the abbot.

Landolfo brought Thomas to this school sometime between July 1230 and May 1231. Thomas was about five or six and was accompanied by his nurse during the trip. It may seem odd to us that he was brought there at such a young age, but that was a normal procedure in those days. Landolfo made a gift of twenty ounces of gold to the monastery, in lieu of a set tuition. The abbot of Monte Cassino was Landolfo Sinibaldi, a distant relative of the Aquinas family.

A studious child with an eager mind for learning, Thomas enjoyed school. He would have followed the typical course of study of the day, which meant studying Latin, grammar, reading, writing, math, and harmony. Monte Cassino was an intense center of learning. The monks transcribed many important manuscripts, not only in theology and philosophy but also works of poetry from the Greeks and Romans. Thomas received not only an academic but also a cultural education, including music and poetry. This foundation served him well later when he composed his famous hymns for the feast of *Corpus Christi*.

With the death of Abbot Sinibaldi around the year 1236, a new abbot, Stephen de Corbario, took over. Things went on as usual in the monastery, but trouble was stirring in the outside world. In his battles with the Church, Emperor Frederick had banished from his kingdom any monks who had not been born there. Since most of the monks at Monte Cassino were from other areas, they had to go, leaving only a few to run the monastery. Thomas stayed there until he had to leave, around 1239, since the monks could no longer staff the school. So he returned to the family castle at Roccasecca.

His time at Monte Cassino left its mark on Thomas. This early familiarity with Benedictine spirituality gave him an appreciation for the monastic life. For example, throughout his life Thomas was fond of reading the *Conferences* of Saint John

Cassian, which contained principles of the ascetical life from the desert fathers. In the *Summa Theologiae,* Thomas cites Cassian over a dozen times.[2] The time Thomas spent in the monastery gave him a solid foundation in the spiritual life.

Thomas didn't stay home for long. His parents wanted him to continue his education, so they sent him to the *studium* at Naples in the fall of 1239. The emperor, Frederick II, had established this center for learning at a time when Italy, and all of Europe in general, was experiencing a great revival of learning and study. The works of the great Greek philosophers, Aristotle in particular, were being translated and circulated. Scholarly Arabic works were being translated as well. We can imagine the young Thomas diving into his studies, his natural eagerness for learning fueled by the heady mix of the new ideas that were being spread.

During his five years in Naples, Thomas studied the liberal arts and philosophy at the Faculty of Arts.

Medieval universities followed an ordered program of study. The liberal arts were divided into two sets: the *trivium,* which consisted of grammar, logic, and rhetoric, and the *quadrivium,* which consisted of arithmetic, geometry, astronomy, and music. In this program, Thomas would have learned skills for correct speech and writing. In his later years as a theologian, he put both of those disciplines to good use, not only in writing but also in his oral disputations and preaching.

Although we don't have a lot of documentation about Thomas from these years, we do know the names of two of his teachers. Master Martin taught him grammar and logic, and Master Peter of Ireland taught him the natural sciences.[3]

The Dominicans

Founded by Saint Dominic, the Order of Preachers (later commonly known as the Dominicans) gained papal approval in 1216. Dominic's passion for preaching the Gospel flowed from his zeal in trying to convert the Albigensians, or Cathars. This heretical group with Gnostic beliefs had been spreading in southern France. Dominic realized that to reach out to them effectively, holy preachers were needed. He dreamed of a group of learned, zealous, and holy priests who would study so as to be able to preach. Thus, the Dominicans were born. They were mendicant preachers, which meant they often traveled, begged for their food, and could move quickly from place to place. The Dominicans valued the intellectual life since their mission of preaching required it. The young Order spread quickly throughout Europe and attracted many candidates.

A Dominican friary had been established at Naples in 1231, and Thomas somehow discovered its existence. Because Frederick II didn't want many mendicants in his empire, by 1239 only two friars lived there, John of San Giuliano and Thomas of Lentini. The latter later became a bishop and was named Patriarch of Jerusalem. Thomas probably saw these friars as they were preaching in the city. Though we don't know the details, he became acquainted with them and grew more and more interested in their life and mission, which was naturally appealing to a devout and studious young man like Thomas. The Dominicans had a freshness about them, that of a new charism[4] in the Church that readily attracted generous young men. Through them Thomas heard the call that Christ directs to young people in every age,

"Come, follow me!" (see Mt 4:19). By now Thomas had been studying in Naples for almost five years. He had probably been praying and reflecting on his vocational calling for some time. In the spring of 1244 he decided to enter the Order of Preachers and received the habit from Thomas of Lentini. But this seemingly simple action would soon ignite a firestorm.

A Family Fight

Thomas' parents already had the idea that he would one day enter the service of the Church. But for them this meant that Thomas would return to Monte Cassino in view of eventually becoming the famous monastery's abbot. After all, they would have thought, a member of the family de Aquino had a certain status. It was only appropriate in their eyes that Thomas should rise to an important position. It would have been a great honor for the family if Thomas had been the abbot at such a renowned center of learning and culture.

As mendicants the Dominicans were the exact opposite of what his family had in mind for his future. The idea of Thomas walking about the countryside begging for food and sleeping in barns with smelly animals revolted them. His mother in particular was upset that Thomas wanted to become a preaching friar. *What?* She must have thought. *Going around the countryside in rough robes, preaching and begging for food? Never would my son lower himself to that!* As soon as she heard the news, Theodora hurried to Naples in hopes of persuading him to abandon this radical idea. Though Thomas' father was still alive, his mother took charge of getting Thomas back. Landolfo was away inspecting his various estates and taking care of business matters. The competent Theodora lost no time as she sprang into action.

But it was too late. The friars knew from previous experience that noble families often did not like the idea of their sons becoming roaming preachers. So they had hurried Thomas out of Naples and sent him to Rome, then on the road toward Bologna. He traveled with John of Wildeshausen, also know as John the Teuton, who was the master general of the Dominicans. Having missed meeting Thomas at Naples, Theodora hurried on to Rome, but by that time Thomas was already gone.

Theodora, however, was a woman who would not easily give up. She sent a messenger to her son Rinaldo, who was a soldier in Frederick's army. Rinaldo was in Acquapendente, an area north of Rome. He took a small force with him and rode off to get Thomas.

The small group of friars were no match for the soldiers, and Rinaldo picked Thomas up easily to carry him back to the family castle. In the scuffle that ensued, however, Thomas adamantly refused to take off his Dominican habit and resisted the soldiers' efforts to tear it off. Although torn and muddied, he was still wearing it when they brought him back to Roccasecca.

Thomas had no intentions of giving up his Dominican vocation. As the story goes, his brothers sent a prostitute to his room to try and tempt him. But Thomas simply chased her out. Then he took a flaming torch, etched a cross on the door of his room, and fell to his knees to pray for the virtue of chastity. Is the story factual? It seems unlikely, though many earlier biographers repeated it.[5] It would not be in keeping with what we know of Theodora to think that she would have approved of this attempt.

Though it is probably only legendary, it is said that after this incident, two angels appeared to Thomas and bound him around his waist with a cord to symbolize chastity. Later, this symbol of the angelic cord would be used as a form of devotion to Saint Thomas, especially to ask his intercession for the virtue of chastity.[6]

Things stood at an impasse. Thomas inherited his mother's determination! He refused to give up his dream of becoming a Dominican. But his family, and his mother in particular, were just as determined to force him to abandon his plans. Back home in the family castle, Thomas was under a sort of house arrest in the sense that he could not freely travel. But he was treated well—it wasn't that he was like a prisoner. Since he had a lot of time on his hands, he put it to good use for study and prayer. He read the entire Bible and studied theology. At that time, taking up theology meant studying the book of *Sentences* of Peter Lombard, the most comprehensive textbook at that time. Thomas began to read this important work, which he would later comment on as a theologian.

The Dominican friar John of San Giuliano visited Thomas in the castle and even brought him a new habit to replace the one that had been torn and dirtied in the scuffle with the soldiers. Thomas also discussed religious topics with his family. He may have even persuaded his sister Marotta to enter the religious life.[7]

After about a year, seeing that Thomas would not budge, his family relented. They let him go back to the Dominicans in Naples. It would have been in the summer of 1245. Despite the conflict, Thomas remained warmly attached to his family. We know from accounts of his later life that he would stay with family members on his travels, and he aided them in certain times of need, such as when he became the executor of his brother-in-law's estate. Thomas had a warm, kind heart that was attentive to the needs of others.

Still, this experience marked Thomas in certain ways for the rest of his life. He had the firm conviction that a person must follow God's will in choosing a vocation and not bow to family pressure. In this regard, an interesting detail sheds some light on how resolute Thomas was.[8] In discussing duties toward one's parents in relation to God, Thomas strongly maintains that parents should not try to thwart religious vocations in their children. He quotes Saint Jerome who wrote to a monk on this topic: "Should your father prostrate himself on the threshold, trample him underfoot (*per calcatum perge patrem*) and go your way. With dry eyes fly to the standard of the cross." But Thomas added a phrase in Latin, *per calcatum perge matrem*—trample one's mother underfoot![9] No doubt he was thinking of Theodora. With these words, he did not mean to say that one should disrespect one's parents, but to put God above all else. Still, his vehemence demonstrates the passion he felt about his own vocation. Since Thomas hardly ever wrote about himself, this is a precious clue that helps us glean something of his personality.

Thomas was now free to follow his vocation. What did the young man think about as he returned to the priory in Naples? He now knew by experience that the journey to God was an arduous road. This episode of his life shows that even as a young man he had remarkable fortitude and a holy stubbornness in doing God's will. Years later, in writing about the virtue of courage, he said, "the chief activity of courage is not so much attacking as enduring, or standing one's ground amidst dangers" (*Summa*, II-II, q. 123, a. 6). Did he perhaps think of his own year in the castle when he wrote that line? Far from being detached from experience, his theology was worked out in the midst of human struggles. With the help of God's grace, he had overcome his first major obstacle. It was only the beginning.

CHAPTER TWO

• • • • • • • • • • •

At Paris and Cologne
with Albert the Great

Thomas didn't stay in Naples for long. With only two friars, the priory was not equipped to train new vocations to the Order. They sent Thomas to Rome, and from there he would proceed to Paris. This move was not only for the purpose of study, but also because the Dominicans wanted to keep him away from his family to avoid further trouble. The master general of the Order, John the Teuton, was passing through Rome on his way to Paris with a small group of friars. Thomas accompanied them on this trip, which took place in the fall of 1245.

In those days, travel was quite arduous. Generally, the friars walked; the Dominicans were not allowed to ride horses, although they could ride a donkey if necessary. Throughout his life, Thomas walked all over Europe. Some have calculated that with all his trips he may have walked as much as nine thousand miles.[1] These long bouts of exercise would have kept him physically fit. On his first trip to Paris he was about twenty years old, and had already grown quite a bit. He was a tall man with a big build. Contrary to popular legend, he was not overweight, much less gluttonous. From the witnesses who testified at his process for canonization, we do know that he was a large man. He had thin hair, with a blondish color like wheat. He had a pleasant, affable disposition and was known for his gentleness and kindness.

Up to this point in his life, Thomas had not been outside Italy. His first trip to Paris, where he would spend much of his life, must have been exciting for the young friar. The Dominican friary in Paris, Saint Jacques, was thriving. Many young men had joined the new Order and were studying in Paris. Though it is not certain, it is likely that when he arrived in Paris, Thomas began his year of novitiate. That first year in Paris was primarily a time of spiritual formation. But since the intellectual life was so much a part of the Dominican tradition from its beginning, Thomas also studied philosophy and possibly some theology. He would have also finished his course of liberal arts.

Albert the Great

Thomas stayed in Paris until the first half of 1248. During that time, he had the great fortune to study under and to get to know Saint Albert the Great. Since their stories are intertwined, some background on Albert would be useful to note here. He was the type of person to whom people would go whenever a question came up. He knew almost everything there was to know in the medieval world. An outstanding philosopher and theologian, he also studied the natural sciences. He painstakingly observed and recorded facts about insects, birds, astronomy, and many other fields.

Born in Germany, Albert entered the recently-founded Order of Preachers sometime in the 1220s. His talents made him an important asset, and he became a professor in Paris and Cologne. At that time, the works of Aristotle were becoming better known in Europe, and Albert took part in the important movement to use the philosopher's thought to better understand Christian doctrine. In this Albert influenced his student, Thomas Aquinas, who went on to develop that field even more. Albert became the provincial of the Dominicans and was appointed bishop of Regensburg in 1260. But being a bishop didn't suit him, and he resigned after three years. He returned to scholarly work and preaching, mainly in Germany. In 1931 Pope Pius XI canonized Albert and made him a Doctor of the Church.

When Thomas was in Paris as a novice, he studied theology with Albert in the Dominican priory, rather than at the University of Paris. Albert quickly noticed the great potential of the young novice. During this time, Thomas also acted as a secretary to Albert. Thomas recopied Albert's commentary *De caelesti hierarchia,* which was a commentary on the work of Pseudo-Dionysius the Areopagite, *The Celestial Hierarchy.* This text on the angels was highly influential in medieval theology and indeed beyond. It had a significant influence on Thomas' own thinking. The manuscript that Thomas copied in his own hand still exists. Ironically, despite his brilliance, Thomas would have failed handwriting. His writing was so bad that it is called the *littera illegibilis,* or "illegible writing"!

Cologne 1248–1252

At their general chapter in June 1248, the Dominicans decided to set up a new *studium generale* in Cologne. The term refers to a school that taught the liberal arts and theology, and was not just for the members of one province but for the whole Order. The chapter asked Albert to start it. It was a natural choice since he was their most prominent theologian. Albert went to Germany with a group of young Dominican friars, including Thomas. They traveled by foot, walking in the summer heat, and probably arrived sometime in August. Thomas may have been present when the foundation stone of the magnificent cathedral of Cologne was put in place on August 15.

In Cologne Thomas continued his studies, prepared for the priesthood, and assisted Albert. Thomas took classes with Albert on such works as the *Divine Names* (of Pseudo-Dionysius the Areopagite) and the *Nicomachean Ethics* (of Aristotle). Even though Thomas had already completed his philosophy program, he took the ethics course probably because he wanted to learn as much as he could from Albert. In these classes Thomas also took notes, which Albert himself later edited and used to write his commentary on Aristotle's ethics.[2]

One of the most famous stories about Thomas comes from this time in his life. By nature, he was quiet and didn't make a show of himself. Because of his silence, and due to his big build, some of his fellow students started calling him "the dumb ox from Sicily." While we might think this meant they thought he was unintelligent, the Latin given by his early biographers reads *boven mutum,* dumb as in mute. One day when Albert walked into class, he heard the students teasing Thomas like this. Albert said, "You call him a dumb ox, but I tell you, one day this ox will bellow so loud that it will resound throughout the whole world."[3]

Another incident from his student days tells us something about Thomas' character. Again, because he was often silent in class, one of the other students thought that Thomas was a bit slow to catch on. So he offered to help him out by trying to explain the *Divine Names* of Pseudo-Dionysius. Thomas amiably agreed. But during their discussion, it soon became apparent that the tutor was struggling with the material himself. Thomas simply explained to him the solution of the problem, and the tutor realized that Thomas certainly didn't need his help! Even if this incident can't be historically verified, the fact that it has been passed down shows what his confreres thought about Thomas. They admired him not just for his genius, but above all for his humility and gentle kindness toward others. For Thomas, his great mind was a gift to be used for the benefit of others, and never as a weapon to cut people down. As he wrote, humility means that "one should put others before oneself."[4]

In the Middle Ages, students of theology would first obtain a bachelor's degree and then a master's. A bachelor had to lecture on the Bible for a year, and then on the *Sentences* of Peter Lombard for two years. A bachelor commenting on the Bible was formally known as a *cursor biblicus,* or "biblical cursor." The name was derived from the way the bachelor worked, that is, to give a cursory explanation of the text, to run over it quickly. It was not the kind of very detailed examination of a text that a master of theology would give. The purpose was to help the students understand the literal meaning of the biblical text, which was the foundation for further study.

While in Cologne, Thomas began teaching as a biblical cursor. In this capacity, he gave lectures on the books of Jeremiah, Lamentations, and part of Isaiah. The latter commentary was more detailed than the others. Thomas wrote these commentaries in his own hand, for they were his own course notes for the lectures. In his commentary on Isaiah, the manuscript of which still exists, Thomas made hasty notes called *collationes* (from the Latin, meaning to bring together, to compare). The notes have to do with spiritual meditations that could be made from the text, which he probably used at a later time for preaching or more devotional activities. In his studies, Thomas never worked merely for an academic purpose. For him, study was the means to grow in knowledge and love of God, and then to pass that on to others. That was the heart of his Dominican charism as a teacher and preacher, one that he lived fully to the end of his life.

Thomas was about twenty-three to twenty-seven years old during the four years he was in Cologne. While there he studied for the priesthood and grew in both learning and holiness. We don't know when he was ordained, but it was probably in Cologne in 1250 or 1251.

In 1252, the master general of the Dominicans, John the Teuton, asked Albert to recommend a promising friar who could go to Paris for further study, to become a bachelor of theology. Being a bachelor of the *Sentences* was an important position on the way to becoming a master of theology. Without any hesitation, Albert recommended Thomas. At first John was reluctant to appoint Thomas, probably because he was still too young. The position required that a friar be at least twenty-nine. But by this time Albert, fully aware of Thomas' genius, used his influence to get his candidate accepted. He appealed to Cardinal Hugh of Saint Cher, who was also a Dominican, to try and persuade John. It worked. Thomas was sent back to Paris. Little did he know that he was walking into a battlefield.

CHAPTER THREE

Teaching in Paris

Paris in the thirteenth century was an incredible center of intellectual life. Its thriving university attracted outstanding teachers and students. It was like a boiling cauldron, however, because controversy was also brewing. The battlefield that Thomas walked into is known as the anti-mendicant controversy. To understand it and how it affected him, we need a little background.

The mendicant Orders, the Dominicans and the Franciscans, were newcomers as far as the university was concerned. Before the mendicants arrived on the scene, the professors were priests who did not belong to religious orders. They were known as the secular masters of theology (secular because they were not bound by the rule of a religious order). The secular masters controlled the university and they were happy with the status quo. When the mendicant friars arrived, however, a turf war ensued. We'll look at the details of this shortly. For now, it is enough to note that when Thomas arrived in Paris, the controversy that was still going on in the background between the seculars and the mendicants was deeply affecting the atmosphere in the university.

Bachelor of the Sentences

Even while continuing his own studies, Thomas began to teach. As a bachelor, he served under a master of theology, the Dominican Elias Brunet. To reach the goal of becoming a master of theology, Thomas had to go through two more stages. First he had to become a bachelor of the *Sentences,* and after that he would become a master of theology. The *Sentences* was the most important theology textbook at that time. It had been put together by the theologian and bishop Peter Lombard in the twelfth century. He collected various statements (*sententiae*) from the Fathers of the Church on the Bible and Catholic doctrine and grouped them into four books. Because these texts dealt with many questions that were still open for debate, the bachelor of theology who commented on them could freely develop his own positions on them. So the various commentaries on the *Sentences* became a focus for theological debates and revealed the talents of the young theologians who commented on them. This practice had first been brought to the University of Paris by Alexander of Hales in the 1220s. From then on, commenting on the *Sentences* was standard procedure for a young theologian in the medieval university. It was an essential part of the preparation that Thomas had to do in order to become a master of theology. Spread out over his four years of teaching from 1252 to 1256, Thomas' commentary was a huge work that came to over five thousand pages. It is still in the process of being translated into English. In this work, Thomas made many original contributions and showed the depth of his thought. He also showed how he was influenced by some important authors, such as Aristotle (over two thousand quotations) and Saint Augustine (about one thousand quotations).[1] Thomas drew much from Augustine. Contrary to what is often thought, there was not such a sharp distinction between Aristotelians and Augustinians in the medieval university.[2]

Thomas' *Commentary on the Sentences* (in Latin, *Scriptum super Sententias)* was not just a transcription of class notes from his lectures taken by someone else (such a work is called a *reportatio*). Instead, Thomas himself wrote and revised this commentary. As Thomas progressed in theology, he would later revise and change some of his opinions as expressed in this commentary. Thomas developed his thought throughout his life, often going deeper into a subject and gaining more profound insights. As one of his biographers notes, "There are many points on which Thomas later abandoned earlier opinions."[3]

During these four years in Paris, Thomas wrote two other minor works called *opuscula*. One was a small treatise titled "On Being and Essence" *(De ente et essentia).* Though short, this was hugely influential because in it Thomas outlined a key position he took in metaphysics. He said that in creatures there is a real distinction between the essence of a thing and its existence. Only in God are essence and existence the same. In other words, for God, his very being is to exist; he is existence itself.

The other small work was called *On the Principles of Nature (De principiis naturae)*. Addressed to an otherwise unknown Brother Sylvester, it deals with matter and form and such things as the four causes.

The Anti-Mendicant Controversy

Sometimes people think of Thomas as teaching peacefully and living a quiet life in the proverbial ivory tower. But just as in our own day when college campuses sometimes break out into protests and demonstrations, the same was true at the University of Paris in the mid 1200s. Coming to a better understanding of the raging controversy will help us better understand Thomas and what he had to deal with.

The Dominicans had first established themselves in Paris in 1218, at the priory of Saint Jacques. In June 1219, Saint Dominic went to Paris to preach and to seek out vocations for his fledgling Order. He succeeded in persuading some of the clerics who taught at the University of Paris to become Dominicans. This was all to the good, but it sowed some seeds for dissension down the line. A little later, Saint Dominic's successor, Jordan of Saxony, also went to Paris to recruit new members. He had extraordinary success, bringing in over one hundred clerics from 1222 to 1236.

In 1229 the first Dominican, Roland of Cremona, became a master of theology at the University of Paris. As a master, he obtained a chair of theology, the first one for the Dominicans. Then in 1230 John of Saint Giles, who was already a master of theology with his own chair at the university, also became a

Dominican while remaining in his position. Now the Dominicans had two chairs of theology. Something similar happened with the Franciscans when another secular master, Alexander of Hales, became a Franciscan and also retained his chair.

The other secular clerics must have looked askance at this development, and resentment started to build. This was fueled by anger at the mendicants for continuing to teach during a strike that the secular masters held in 1229–1230. The university had a limited number of chairs of theology, so giving them to the mendicants meant that the secular masters had fewer. Naturally they wanted to retain their influence, so some were not so happy to see the chairs go to the mendicants.

Thus the anti-mendicant controversy began to brew, and it would continue for some time. While it certainly had elements of a turf war, there was much more to it than that. It had another dimension: the mendicants had been given certain privileges by the pope that allowed them to preach and to hear confessions wherever they wanted to. Unlike secular clerics, the friars didn't have to get permission from the local bishop, so that they would be free enough to fulfill their new mission in the Church. But their privileges caused some problems with the local bishops, who wanted some measure of control over the priests working in their dioceses. Because the friars had these special privileges from the pope, some resentment over them grew up even outside the university.

To understand all this, we need to remember that the mendicants were a new phenomenon in the Church at that time. They were founded to meet the pastoral needs of the day, so the friars went out preaching and teaching. They were not bound to monasteries as monks were. It took some time for people to get used to this idea.

When Thomas came to Paris in 1252, the Dominicans had two chairs and the Franciscans had one. Beginning in 1252 the controversy began to swirl even more intensely. Like a tornado, it swept up people and shook the academic halls of Paris. It can easily become confusing to follow all the details, but our main interest here is how it affected Thomas. The main lines of the controversy ran like this: in February 1252, the seculars tried to take away the Dominicans' second chair of theology. They declared this by way of a statute, but the friars resisted.

In the summer of that year, Thomas arrived in Paris and began teaching as a bachelor of the *Sentences*. From 1252 to 1256, the four years he taught there, the anti-mendicant controversy became more heated.

In April 1253 the seculars went on strike over various grievances that they blamed on the mendicants, but the mendicant masters did not join them on the strike. So the seculars issued a decree saying the mendicant masters were excommunicated. In response, the friars appealed to the Pope, protesting the unfair penalty.

In July 1253 Pope Innocent IV ruled in favor of the mendicants, removed the penalty of excommunication, and reinstated the mendicants in their chairs of theology.

Early in 1254, a Franciscan named Gerard de Borgo San Donnino published a book promoting the erroneous ideas of Joachim of Fiore. Joachim had said a new age of the Holy Spirit had begun, one that basically did away with the need for the sacraments. This provided the fodder needed by William of

Saint-Amour, one of the secular masters who was an ardent opponent of the mendicants. William became the loudest voice protesting the mendicants.

He wrote a rebuttal of Gerard's book and took the matter to the Pope. Taking advantage of this opportunity to press his case against the mendicants, William persuaded the Pope to revoke their special privileges regarding preaching and hearing confessions. But only two weeks after this, Pope Innocent IV died (December 7, 1254). His successor, Pope Alexander IV, lost no time in rescinding Innocent's order. He not only restored the mendicants' privileges but also commanded that the two Dominican masters be reinstated at the University of Paris.

But the controversy was far from over. William did not accept defeat even at the hands of the Pope. He continued his campaign to discredit the friars, using whatever means he could: by preaching, holding disputations, and organizing student protests. Some violence even broke out in the streets. The friars could not go out and beg as they usually did. Things got so heated that on one occasion in 1255, when the Dominican Florent of Hesdin was scheduled to give his inaugural lecture as a master, King Louis IX had to send the royal archers to protect the friars from the angry mob.

William also put his pen to work against the friars. In March 1256, he published his most famous work against the friars, *De periculis novissimorum temporum* (*On the Dangers of Recent Times*). He attacked them on many grounds, saying that they shouldn't be out preaching, hearing confessions, begging, teaching, etc. This screed was a frontal assault on the very rights of the mendicants to exist in the Church.

Such an attack could not go unanswered. By the summer of that year, Saint Bonaventure had written a well-reasoned response. A little later, in October 1256, Thomas wrote his own response, a treatise called "A Defense of the Religious Orders."[4]

Thomas took up all the objections of William and responded to them in detail. In his writing, Thomas is usually very objective and dispassionate. Here, however, he was defending the very way of life to which he had dedicated himself. Thus the treatise is charged with a certain emotional intensity that is unusual for Thomas. For example, he writes, "In our attempt to check the calumnies of these foul tongues, we shall proceed in the following order." And toward the end of the treatise he writes, "Much might still be said in confutation of the detractors of religious. But we will leave them to the Divine judgment, since the malice of their heart is clearly revealed by the speech that falls from their lips."[5] This intensity gives us an insight into Thomas the man, who reacted with vigor to defend the Order he so loved.

Also in October 1256, the Pope condemned William's treatise. It is very unlikely that Thomas knew about that, however, since news traveled slowly in those days. With the papal condemnation, William didn't have much to stand on. He continued to try and make trouble for the friars, but he had lost the battle. The next year, in 1257, King Louis sent William back to his home village of Saint-Amour. On August 9, 1257, Pope Alexander wrote a letter excommunicating William. His most important followers accepted the Pope's rulings. Things were beginning to quiet down, though new troubles would erupt about ten years later.

But the controversy had far wider significance.[6] William failed to understand what the new mendicant orders were all about. He viewed their members as monks, who should stay in monasteries and not travel about the countryside. But the Orders had been started to respond to the great pastoral needs of the day. The Church needed these friars who would go about the countryside preaching the Gospel. This response to contemporary needs had been inspired by the Holy Spirit, which was why the mendicants ultimately prevailed. It was as if William was fighting a sort of rear guard action to bring things back to the way they had been a century earlier. But times had changed. The friars were there to stay.

Master of the Sacred Page

Thomas continued in his role as bachelor of the *Sentences* despite the controversy raging around him. He was still aiming for his goal of becoming a master of theology. This process required that the bachelor successfully lecture on the *Sentences* in order to receive his license to teach (the *licentia docendi*). The chancellor of the University, Aimeric of Veire, supported Thomas and awarded him this license to teach. But his acceptance as a master also had to be submitted for papal approval, and Pope Alexander approved it in a bull dated March 3, 1256.

At that time, Thomas was about thirty-one or thirty-two years old. A master had to be thirty-five, so Thomas' concern was that he might not be ready to take on this responsibility. He would have to give his lecture in September 1256. As he always did whenever something troubled him, he prayed much about it.

Then something a unusual happened. This incident is well verified, since Thomas himself later told the story to Friar Reginald,
his assistant, and three different sources also attest to it.[7]

One night Thomas had a dream in which a venerable, older-
looking Dominican friar approached him to ask what Thomas
was so worried about. He replied that to become a master of theology, he had to give a special inaugural lecture, and he didn't
know what to talk about. The older friar suggested that he speak
about Psalm 104:13, "From your lofty abode you water the
mountains; the earth is satisfied with the fruit of your work"
(NRSV).[8] Though we don't know if Thomas ever said who the
friar was, the Dominicans generally thought it must have been
Saint Dominic himself.

So Thomas based his lecture on that text. He used the image
of God watering the mountains as a metaphor, seeing it as the
communication of divine wisdom. Thomas spoke of the nature
of divine wisdom itself, the role of its teacher, the students who
receive it, and how to communicate it. This short text shows us
how Thomas understood his own role as a master of theology,
which at that time meant to be a "master of the sacred page," that
is, Scripture. In this lecture, Thomas uses Scripture very adeptly
to illustrate and drive home his points. Above all else, as a theologian Thomas was dedicated to the exposition of Scripture. As
we will see, he identifies the teaching of theology with the teaching of Scripture. Although Thomas is perhaps best known for his
Summas and philosophical works, we shouldn't forget that he
also authored a number of important Biblical commentaries.
Somewhat neglected, these commentaries are vitally important
to understanding Thomas as a theologian.

Besides his inaugural lecture, Thomas also had to submit four questions for discussion by other professors, and then he would have to conclude the discussion by summarizing all of the arguments and giving his own solution to the problem. That wasn't as easy as it might appear, for the new masters were thoroughly grilled by the others, who spared no efforts to complicate things. The medieval masters were experts at debating disputed questions. We can only imagine how relieved Thomas was when that ordeal was over and he was officially installed as a new master. From then on his teaching duties became even more intense, duties that Thomas always fulfilled with great generosity and love.

Even as Thomas delivered his inaugural lecture, the anti-mendicant controversy continued. Some of the friars' opponents made trouble for those who wished to listen to their lectures. Apparently this even happened when Thomas gave his lecture, as the following excerpt from a letter of Pope Alexander IV indicates:

> The aforesaid masters and students have had no care, as we well know, to preserve that concord which the thorns of discord have assailed. They have opposed in the most unworthy manner those who desired to attend the lectures, disputations, and sermons of the friars, and in particular those who wished to be present at the inaugural lecture of our beloved son Father Thomas d'Aquino.[9]

Although Thomas began teaching as a master, he wasn't formally accepted into the *consortium* of the masters for another sixteen months. In August 1257 both he and Bonaventure were fully accepted. These events can help us see that Thomas' life as a scholar could be difficult. Despite the opposition, he carried out his teaching mission with great dedication.

A Day in the Life of Thomas

At this point, what did Thomas' daily life look like? Thomas' typical day as a master of theology was taken up largely by prayer and teaching. He would get up early and pray, then celebrate Mass. After that he would usually be present for the Mass of the friar who served as his secretary. A light breakfast followed, and then he would begin his busy day of teaching and studying. The master of theology had three main tasks: to lecture, to dispute, and to preach.

Lecture

What did the master lecture on? The Bible. In fact, it's important to know that for the great medieval masters of theology, the Bible held primacy of place. The very first question of the *Summa Theologiae* underlines this important point. Thomas identifies theology with the study of the sacred page, or the Bible. In this question he discusses what sacred teaching is, and from his answers it is evident that he equates sacred teaching with the Bible.

In lecturing, the master of theology would take one of the books of the Bible and study it in detail. First he would read it, then he would show how it was divided into various parts, and then he would go through it line by line, commenting on it in great detail. This was not done in isolation but in conjunction with reading other texts that related to it, such as the writings of the Fathers of the Church and the Gloss. Held in great esteem, the Gloss was a sort of commentary on Scripture. It consisted of citations from the Fathers or other authorities that were often written in the margin of the Biblical book.

Questions would often arise while doing this. Sometimes various patristic authorities might seem to contradict each other, or some other problem would be seen. The master would comment on these and show how to reach a good solution to such difficulties.

This reading and commenting on the Bible generally took the whole morning. During his years of teaching, Thomas commented on a little over half of the books of the New Testament, as well as some of the Old Testament books. These scriptural commentaries of Thomas have come down to us in two ways.

The first type is called a *reportatio.* This is a record of the lecture that was taken down by someone other than the master who was present at the time. Most of Thomas' commentaries on Scripture are *reportatios,* such as Matthew, John, part of First Corinthians, Hebrews (ch. 11 to the end), some of the Psalms, and a few other texts.

The second type is called an *ordinatio.* This is more valuable in that the master himself either wrote or dictated it. Only a few of Thomas' scriptural commentaries are of this type, such as the first eight chapters of Romans and First Corinthians from 1:1 to 7:9. However, many of his other works are in this category, such as all the commentaries on Aristotle, the disputed questions, the *Summa Theologiae,* and the *Summa Contra Gentiles.*

These scriptural commentaries of Thomas were rather neglected for a long time, and English translations were not

readily available.[10]   More recently, however, interest in them
has been renewed. They are essential reading in order to get a
well-rounded view of Thomas the theologian. A different type
of genre from the *Summa Theologiae,* they give insights into
Thomas that we wouldn't get if we only read the *Summa.* His
commentaries on Matthew, John, and Romans, in particular,
are beautiful and profound. Anyone who reads them will notice
a few things:

1.   Thomas abundantly quoted Scripture in order to inter-
     pret it. He evidently knew the whole Bible very well and
     seamlessly wove texts from both the Old and the New
     Testaments into any book he commented on. This gives
     the reader a greater sense of the unity of all Scripture and
     how the various books are interrelated.

2.   He also used various interpretations of the Fathers of the
     Church. When they might have a different understand-
     ing of a text, Thomas acknowledged this and would say,
     for example, "Augustine understands this text different-
     ly . . ." and then he would explain that. He often left the
     interpretation open-ended, in that he didn't try to tell
     the reader that only one interpretation was correct.

3.   Thomas also was concerned to present the teachings
     of the Church as they flow from Scripture. He quoted
     councils, and he also mentioned various errors proposed
     by different people in order to correct them. For exam-
     ple, in commenting on Romans 1:3 concerning Jesus as
     the "Son of God with power," Thomas went through sev-
     eral of the early Christological heresies and showed why

they were wrong. His explanation of the text is quite thorough and gives the reader a good understanding of the mystery of the incarnation.

Keep in mind that Thomas' way of presenting Scripture was very different from the methods of modern Scripture scholars. And Thomas remained Thomas, the philosopher and theologian who thought in the categories of his medieval world. For example, in commenting on the words of Christ in chapter 6 of John's Gospel, Thomas said, "His major premise is . . . His minor premise is . . . And His conclusion is . . ." It would be a rare Scripture scholar today who would put the words of Christ into a syllogism! Certainly, we need to take account of the fruits of modern studies. But Thomas' approach can also teach us much, for he looks on the word of God not only as a source for theology but as food for our souls.

Dispute

After lecturing in the morning, in the afternoon Thomas would turn to the dispute. This was an important part of teaching in the medieval university. In the dispute, questions would be proposed, objections put forth, and the master would then resolve the dispute by giving a solution to the problem.

The dispute could be either public or private. The private disputes were held with the master, his bachelor, and his students. It was an important part of how a subject was taught, because the students were trained not only to raise difficulties but also to consider the objections and come up with solutions. These disputes involved a great deal of discussion between the master and his students. We can imagine Thomas engaged in these discussions, always wanting to help his students grow in their knowledge. For him, teaching was not an exercise in which the students were merely like sponges, soaking up information but not challenged to think on their own. Instead, Thomas wrote that the purpose of these disputed questions was

> . . . less to push error out than to lead listeners into the truth they strive to understand. Accordingly they must be carried by reasonings in order to get to the root of the matter, and helped to see for themselves how what is asserted is true. Otherwise, if the appeal is merely to bare authorities, then all the teacher does is to certify to his listeners that such in fact is the answer to the problem; apart from this they have gathered no reason for it and no understanding, and so go empty away.[11]

Thomas would have engaged in these disputes on the days that he taught. He strove not to score points but to help his students achieve a deeper understanding of theology. An important part of the learning process was to examine and critically discuss the positions put forward by various theologians of the past and of the day. Thomas was always confident that since the human mind is made for truth, these discussions would enable his students to distinguish between true and false ideas.

The public disputes were held every year during Lent and Advent. They were called *quodlibets* (meaning "whatever pleases" in Latin) because anyone who attended was free to raise any question at all. In these debates, Thomas was putting himself on the spot, since he didn't know in advance what questions would be raised. Both students and other masters could attend, and sometimes they would challenge him with very complex questions. While the *quodlibets* were going on, regular classes were not held. So Thomas would have spent his whole academic day in these discussions.

Although they are not as well known as his two *Summas,* we have quite a few of the disputed questions that Thomas dealt with, for example his *Disputed Questions on Truth.* This work contains questions from his private disputes, not the *quodlibets*, so Thomas was able to develop a particular theme. During the discussions, a secretary would take notes. Later, Thomas went over these notes, made corrections, and developed various points. This insured that he would cover the subject matter in detail and in an organized way. The text of these disputed questions is much more involved than that of the *Summa Theologiae.* While the *Summa* usually has about three objections per question, the disputed questions have many more.

Preach

Besides lecturing and disputing, a master was required to preach. Thomas was assigned to preach a certain number of sermons at the University of Paris during the scholastic year. Unfortunately, only a few of these have come down to us. He also preached at his own Dominican priory.[12] Usually that was either on a Sunday or a feast day, so Thomas would not teach on those days. He would preach a sermon in the morning, and then give a conference or extended reflection (called a collation) for the evening vespers service. A wonderful example of a sermon and collation that Thomas preached for Pentecost is available online.[13] We also have some other sermons that Thomas preached later in his life in Naples. These were addressed to lay people, and Thomas adapted his style to suit his listeners. In these sermons he preached about the Creed, the Our Father, and the Hail Mary. He does not go into difficult theological points, but covers the basics in a way the people could easily understand. He preached these during Lent, and it is said that crowds of people came to hear this humble and learned friar.

Sometimes Thomas had unfriendly listeners too. Once when Thomas was preaching at the University of Paris on Palm Sunday in 1259, a university student named Guillot interrupted Thomas and started to heckle him. Guillot was an anti-mendicant and tried to use this as an opportunity to embarrass a Dominican. Undoubtedly Thomas handled this with his usual grace and defused the situation.

His lectures, disputes, and preaching kept Thomas quite busy. But apart from all this, he also carried out duties in service of the Dominican Order. This required him to attend certain meetings, including general chapters. The chapters were larger meetings with Dominicans from various provinces. It gave the friars an opportunity to discuss how things were going in the Order and what areas they could develop. The chapter could also commission certain friars to do particular tasks, as Thomas would soon experience.

Chapter Four

· · · · · · · · · · · ·

Return to Italy and More Writing

Thomas attended the general chapter of the Dominicans that was held at Valenciennes, France, in June 1259. While there he was part of a commission that was tasked with developing a program to promote studies in the Dominican Order. The commission also included Albert the Great and some other top-notch Dominican scholars.

Shortly after the general chapter Thomas headed back to Italy, having finished his term as a master of theology in Paris. At that time, the Dominicans were anxious to train as many friars as possible to be masters of theology. So, unlike the modern-day practice of tenure, the masters of theology were rotated as much as possible. The Dominicans wanted to place their friars wherever they could do the most good. From 1259 to 1261, Thomas continued writing, teaching, and developing his theology.

Thomas was the first master of theology for the Dominicans of Italy, so they valued his expertise. In 1260 he was made a preacher general for the priory at Naples. Being a preacher general carried certain privileges, such as the right to vote in the provincial chapters. In this way his fellow Dominicans were assured that they would have his valuable input at their chapters. These meetings were held every year in different cities throughout Italy. Thomas attended them all, which required a lot of traveling.

Friar Reginald of Piperno

Upon his return to Italy Thomas was given a *socius,* Friar Reginald of Piperno. The *socius* was an assistant who helped the master of theology, who took dictation as a secretary but also helped the master in other ways. He would serve at Thomas' Mass and probably helped him with personal details. Thomas doesn't seem to have been greatly concerned about his clothing or possessions, except for books. He was often abstracted, lost in his thoughts, so it seems likely that mundane details like rumpled clothing were not important to him. Reginald would have helped him even with those things, almost like a valet. Every genius needs someone to keep him grounded when it comes to the everyday details of life.

Reginald was a Dominican friar and something of a scholar in his own right. He was well matched with Thomas and would remain his friend and associate for the rest of Thomas' life. He was also one of the few people who could actually read Thomas' handwriting.

The Summa Contra Gentiles

In Paris Thomas had begun an important project that he brought with him to finish in Italy: the *Summa Contra Gentiles*. Along with his *Summa Theologiae,* this book is one of Thomas' better-known works. Written in four books with many short chapters, it is much smaller than his other *Summa.* It is also precious because we have much of it written in Thomas' own hand, his famous *littera illegibilis.* Both the date and the purpose of this work have been the subject of much controversy. Even today scholars present different ideas about this. The date, however, has become much more certain. Studies of the parchment and the ink he used indicate that Thomas wrote the first fifty-three chapters in Paris before mid-1259, and it's generally thought that he completed the work in Italy by 1265–1267.[1]

Thomas' purpose in writing the *Summa Contra Gentiles* is also the subject of debate. Traditionally the story was that Saint Raymond of Peñafort, who was working as a missionary in Spain among the Moors, asked Thomas for a manual that could be used to dialogue with non-Christians, and the Muslims in particular. But historical studies have shown there is no strong foundation for this story. While scholars may argue about the specific circumstances that occasioned the writing of this book, it is clear from the work itself that Thomas wished to present the truth of the Catholic faith in a way suited to convince non-believers.

A passage toward the beginning reveals something about Thomas the man and how he thought about his own life and mission:

And so, in the name of the divine Mercy, I have the confidence to embark upon the work of a wise man, even though this may surpass my powers, and I have set myself the task of making known, as far as my limited powers will allow, the truth that the Catholic faith professes, and of setting aside the errors that are opposed to it. To use the words of Hilary: "I am aware that I owe this to God as the chief duty of my life, that my every word and sense may speak of Him" (*De Trinitate* I, 37).[2]

In passages like this, Thomas' humility becomes evident. He was not pretending that on his own powers he could explain the truth about God. We find here the missionary task of his life, why he can be called a missionary of truth. In quoting Saint Hilary, Thomas was even saying that this was how he saw the chief task of his life. It was what he was all about: with all his might, with all his powers, to make the truth about God known to all—the truth taught by the Catholic faith.

Orvieto

The town of Orvieto would play an important role in Thomas' life for the next few years. Located about seventy-five miles north of Rome, this small city is built on top of a high mountain. Visitors to the city today have to ride a tram up the very steep mountainside made of huge rocky cliffs. Thomas, of course, would have had to climb up on foot.

The Dominicans had a priory in Orvieto, and in 1261 Thomas was assigned there to be the lector. He took up residence there in September or October of that year. A new pope had just been elected, Urban IV. In 1262 Urban moved to the papal palaces in Orvieto. He and Thomas would become good friends.

As lector, Thomas had the duty to lecture to the Dominican community on Scripture. He could choose any book, and he chose to lecture on the Book of Job, focusing on the theme of Divine Providence. Thomas was writing on the same topic in his *Summa Contra Gentiles* at that time (Book III), so the two texts dovetailed nicely.

Thomas' Discovery of Greek Theology

An important theological development occurred for Thomas while he was working in Orvieto: he discovered the riches of Greek theology in his study of the Eastern Fathers of the Church.

Pope Urban had asked Thomas to compose a gloss on the four Gospels. This gloss would consist of quotations from the various Church writers who had commented on the Gospels. Thomas went verse by verse through the Gospels, laboriously assembling this magnificent collection of quotations by the best theological writers. This work is called the *Golden Chain* (*Catena Aurea*), a beautiful, woven tapestry bringing together an incredibly rich series of reflections on the Gospel. In doing this work, Thomas also mined the riches of the Eastern writers. This opened his eyes to the treasures he could find there, and it marked a turning point in the development of his theology.

Why didn't he do that before? In our age of the internet where we have instant access to virtually unlimited texts, it can be hard for us to imagine a world where printed texts were very precious and hard to come by. One story about Thomas says that once when he was in Paris, he was traveling with a group of friars outside the city. From their vantage point they turned and could see the entire city before them. One of the friars asked Thomas in good humor if he wouldn't like to be lord of the city. Thomas demurred, saying that he would rather have a copy of Saint John Chrysostom's sermons on the Gospel of Matthew. Thomas actively sought out texts of the ancient Church writers for their content so that he could use original sources as much as possible. He didn't have access to texts of the ancient Church writers from the beginning of his theological career, but as he traveled, and as more texts were made available, he used them as much as possible.

Another important discovery for him was the acts and proceedings of the early ecumenical councils of the Church. He discovered these in the early 1260s, either at the library of Monte Cassino or the papal archives in Orvieto. These were very important, as he used them to clarify and develop his theology, especially on questions concerning the Holy Trinity and the procession of the Holy Spirit. He also relied on them in his masterful treatment of Christology in the third part of the *Summa Theologiae*.

Pseudo-Dionysius

One of the authors Thomas respected very much was Pseudo-Dionysius. This author held great authority in the Middle Ages because he was thought to be the same Dionysius who had been Saint Paul's convert in Athens (see Acts 17:34).

But in fact he was not. Pseudo-Dionysius was probably Syrian and wrote in the early sixth century. At times he had also been confused with Saint Denis, who was the third-century martyr and bishop of Paris.

Thomas had heard Albert the Great's lectures on *The Celestial Hierarchy* of Pseudo-Dionysius and had even helped Albert copy his notes on that text, which later served as an important source for Thomas' writing on the angels. Thomas wrote his own commentary on another work of Pseudo-Dionysius called *On the Divine Names* (*De divinis nominibus*). The date of this commentary is uncertain, but Thomas wrote it sometime during his stay in Italy, probably before 1268.

Pseudo-Dionysius was a mystical writer influenced by Neoplatonism, which tried to integrate Plato's teachings with Christian thought. Through this channel Thomas gleaned certain Platonic ideas that enriched his thought. While Thomas is usually considered much more of an Aristotelian, he was not exclusively so. He certainly drew many elements of his philosophy from Aristotle, but he also used other sources such as Pseudo-Dionysius. This reminds us that the complexity of Thomas' thought can't be neatly reduced to certain categories.

The Feast of Corpus Christi

Besides his great theological work, Thomas was also a great poet and writer of hymns. His best known work in this regard has to do with the feast of *Corpus Christi*, first celebrated in 1246 in the diocese of Liège (present day Belgium). Under the inspiration of a devout group of women headed by Saint Julienne of

Mont-Cornillon, the bishop Robert of Torote approved their request to establish a feast in honor of the Body and Blood of Christ. It started as a local celebration but soon began to spread. The Dominican Hugh of Saint-Cher approved it for use in Germany, where he was the cardinal-legate.

On August 11, 1264, Pope Urban IV established the feast for the whole Church through the publication of the papal bull *Transiturus.* Before becoming pope, Urban had been in Liège and knew Saint Julienne, so he was well acquainted with the background of the feast. However, in Italy the impetus for the feast originated with the Eucharistic miracle at Bolsena, a small town near Orvieto. A priest who was traveling through the area and who had been experiencing doubts about the Eucharist celebrated Mass in the town. During Mass the Sacred Host began to bleed, and the doubting priest reaffirmed his faith. The corporal he used at the Mass is now venerated in the cathedral in Orvieto, which is a magnificent example of Siennese Gothic architecture. This miracle stirred up popular Eucharistic devotion. Pope Urban asked Thomas to write the texts for the Mass and Office of this feast. This includes some of his most famous hymns that are still sung today and cherished by Catholics, such as the *Pange lingua, Tantum ergo,* and *Panis angelicus.* Although for a while some scholars had expressed doubts that Thomas was the author of the liturgical texts, more recent studies have concluded without a doubt that he indeed was the author.[3] The theology of the texts is like Thomas' autograph, since some of the wording he used has a close resemblance to the theological language he used in his other writings.

Although the feast was set for the Thursday following the octave of Pentecost, that first year it was celebrated in Orvieto in the late summer of 1264. Pope Urban died shortly after, on October 2. The implementation of the feast was never fully carried out until 1317 under Pope John XXII. The feast grew in popularity and is still celebrated today, sometimes with outdoor processions and adoration of the Blessed Sacrament.

CHAPTER FIVE

Rome and the Beginning of the *Summa Theologiae*

Thomas attended the provincial chapters each year when he was in Italy. In September 1265, the provincial chapter gave him the mandate to establish a *studium* at Rome. This would be a house of studies for the young friars in formation. At that time many young men were joining the Dominicans, and the intellectual formation of these students was a pressing matter. Since preaching was at the heart of their Dominican vocation, they needed adequate studies. It seems that the *studium* was not a large-scale project, as were the *studia generalia*—larger facilities with more faculty. Instead, this smaller school could even be considered a personal project of Thomas. It was located at the Dominican priory next to the Church of Santa Sabina, which dates from the fifth century. Situated on the Aventine Hill, the church offers a magnificent view of Rome. Today a garden of orange trees grows next to the church. The fragrant orange blossoms add to the loveliness of the area.

Thomas arrived in Rome in the midst of great political turmoil. A long-standing conflict between the Hohenstaufens (a dynasty of German kings) and the kingdom of Naples was still going on. The Hohenstaufens threatened papal territory. Pope Urban IV had appealed to King Louis IX of France for help, but the king was busy preparing to go on crusade in the Holy Land, so he sent Charles of Anjou in his place. A few years later, in 1268, Conradin (the grandson of Frederick II) also got involved in the ongoing conflict and came to Rome. Some of his men looted the Church of Santa Sabina while Thomas was living at the friary. Fortunately, the Dominicans were not harmed. People may mistakenly think Thomas lived a placid academic life, reading dusty, ancient manuscripts, but he had to face life's troubles as we all do.

Course of Studies

In his two years at the *studium* in Rome, what did Thomas teach? He started with the *Sentences* of Peter Lombard. This material, however, proved too hard for the students who did not have advanced studies. As we will shortly see, that was one reason why Thomas wrote his *Summa Theologiae*. It's likely that Thomas also lectured on *The Divine Names* by Dionysius and, of course, on the Bible.

Thomas also held disputations, though these were not as elaborate as the debates held in Paris. As a teacher, Thomas was dedicated to helping his students learn thoroughly, and that included hearing all sides of a disputed question. "It was not enough to hear the great books of Western thought expounded by a master; it was essential that the great ideas be examined critically in the disputation . . . the disputation could not be totally neglected without prejudice to learning."[1] The disputations that Thomas engaged in are proof of how dedicated he was to the pursuit of truth. He lived in a lively world of deep thought and critical debate. The medieval world was certainly a world of deep faith, but that doesn't mean it was a world of stagnant thought, as some might think. Medieval scholars believed in bringing ideas out into the open, to be discussed and critically considered.

While not all of Thomas' works can be dated precisely, it is generally accepted that the following works originated as disputations during his time at the *studium* in Rome:

- *On the Power of God (De potentia Dei)*, which concerns questions on God's power and governance of the universe (1265–1266).
- *On the Soul (De anima)*, which studies the nature of the soul, its powers, the intellect, the soul's union with the body, and related matter (1265–1266).[2]
- *On Spiritual Creatures (De spiritualibus creaturis)*, which discusses angels, human souls, and their relationships (Nov. 1267 to Sept. 1268).

The Summa Theologiae

In his short life, Thomas was an astonishingly prolific writer. But without a doubt his most famous work is the *Summa*

Theologiae. It is an incredible achievement, one that stands out in Catholic theology; it has no equal. Thomas never finished it, having died while it was still in progress. Since it is such a significant work, it is worth looking at it in a bit more detail. First we will look at its content, and then at the reasons Thomas decided to write it. (See the appendix on page 103 for more information on the *Summa Theologiae.*)

Plan of the Summa

The *Summa* is divided into three parts. Part One (*prima pars*) covers God and creation. Thomas discusses the existence of God, the three Persons of the Trinity, creation, the angels, human beings, human intelligence, human beings made in the image of God, and how God governs the universe.

Part Two covers the moral life and is subdivided into two parts. In the first part (*prima secundae*) Thomas starts by considering happiness and the purpose of life. This leads him to the topics of human psychology and principles of morality, including factors such as the passions that can lead us toward or away from good. In the second part (*secunda secundae*) he offers a comprehensive treatment of the moral life built around the search for happiness through virtue. Starting with the theological virtues of faith, hope, and charity, Thomas continues with the cardinal virtues of prudence, justice, fortitude, and temperance.

He explains what each virtue is, considers its parts and allied virtues, and any sins opposed to it. He correlates each of the seven virtues named above with one of the gifts of the Holy Spirit and also a beatitude. By basing his approach on virtue and grace,

Thomas gives a very refreshing account of the moral life. For him it is not a matter of rules but of what God has written into our nature, and the understanding that if we follow it, we will find happiness.

Part Three (*tertia pars*) covers the incarnation and the mysteries of the life, death, and resurrection of Jesus Christ. Thomas wrote about the sacraments in general, and specifically on Baptism, Confirmation, the Holy Eucharist, and Penance. But he died before he could finish this part. Some of his confreres added a supplement drawn from his earlier writings to fill in the parts he had intended to cover.

Structure of the Summa Theologiae

Thomas delves into this material by asking questions. The *Summa* contains 512 questions, which are subdivided into articles—2,669 of them! Each article has several objections to which Thomas responds. In all, he considered about ten thousand objections and their replies. In this way, he systematically treated all the topics he had arranged.

Apart from the specific material he treats, we could learn from Thomas a wonderful openness to the ideas of others, along with critical thinking. When he looked at a question, Thomas considered the best objections to the position he would take on that question. Many of these objections were derived from real objections given by other thinkers. He also derived them from his experience of the disputations. Then he would carefully consider each one and respond to it. In so much of today's politically correct discourse, whether political or otherwise, it can be hard to find a reasoned consideration of all sides of an issue. Often, instead, emotions take over and people who hold divergent views are sometimes even called "haters" or "deniers." This is absurd, a way of shutting down critical thought by labeling other people instead of grappling with their ideas. While Thomas never hesitated to disagree with views he thought false, he never attacked the people who held those views. He didn't call them names. The closest he came was when he said the opinion of a certain David of Dinant was *stultissimus*—which could be loosely translated as "really stupid."[3] But even then, Thomas was talking about David's opinion, not David himself.

Thomas' overall structure for the *Summa*—and teaching theology in general—started with God, then creation, the human person as an image of God, the Fall, virtues and the moral life, the incarnation, and, finally, the sacraments, through which we return to God. This approach is sometimes called *exitus-reditus* (going out and coming back).

Why Did Thomas Write the Summa?

The main reason was that he wanted to have a textbook for teaching theology to the Dominican students that would not be too hard for them to understand. In his foreword to the *Summa* Thomas states: "Because the doctor of Catholic truth ought not only to teach the proficient, but also to instruct beginners (according to the Apostle: *As unto little ones in Christ, I gave you milk to drink, not meat* [1 Cor 3:1–2]) we purpose in this book to treat of whatever belongs to the Christian religion, in such a way as may tend to the instruction of beginners."[4]

The "beginners" he refers to are those students. In 1265, when he first began teaching at the *studium* in Rome, he realized that the Lombard's *Sentences* and his own commentary on them were too difficult for his students to comprehend. They didn't have enough background in philosophy and theology to follow it. Thomas also states:

> We have considered that students in this doctrine have not seldom been hampered by what they have found written by other authors, partly on account of the multiplication of useless questions, articles, and arguments, partly also because those things that are needful for them to know are not taught according to the order of the subject matter, but according as the plan of the book might require, or the occasion of the argument offer, partly, too, because frequent repetition brought weariness and confusion to the minds of readers.[5]

The useless questions and articles could refer to the many objections that were raised in the publicly disputed questions. It would become weary and tiresome for students to wade through all of that. Sometimes the points were so minute that they did little to further the students' understanding.

The *Summa* would offer several advantages: it would be systematic so that all points of doctrine could be considered in an organic whole; it would use only the best objections, so the students wouldn't get bogged down in useless minutiae; and it would be clear and to the point, as Thomas could always be.

The important thing for us to note here is what the *Summa* tells us about Thomas as a teacher. He was concerned first of all for the good of his students. He was looking for what would be in their best interests, not his.

Thomas began writing the *Summa* in 1266, in Rome, and finished the first part by the fall of 1268, but the project of writing the *Summa* would occupy him for the rest of his life. It's not that he wrote it all from scratch, however. He used material that he had developed while teaching, especially some of his disputations. The three disputations mentioned earlier served as the basis for much of the first part of the *Summa:* The book *On the Power of God* concerns God's attributes; *On the Soul* concerns the human person and intelligence, and *On Spiritual Creatures* concerns angels and human beings.[6] But keep in mind that Thomas also developed his thought as he went along. For example, the book *On the Power of God* shows a development of Thomas' thought about God's action in creating, which stands midway between the *Summa Contra Gentiles* and the *Summa Theologiae.*[7] Thomas was always thinking, studying, and praying. His reflective mind always sought out new aspects of a topic so that his understanding of it grew, and this is evidenced in his own writings.

Thomas and His Vocation

An incident that happened around 1267 sheds even more light on how Thomas viewed his vocation. The pope at the time, Clement IV, offered Thomas the bishopric of Naples. His biographers tell us that Thomas had no desire to become a bishop, so he declined the Pope's offer. Thomas also begged him not to ask him to take up any type of office again. Thomas saw his call from God as being a teaching friar, a Dominican who dedicated himself to study not for his own sake, but for that of others. He was not just a scholar, but a teacher who wanted to give to others what he had learned through both study and prayer. As he said, "For even as it is better to enlighten than merely to shine, so is it better to give to others the fruits of one's contemplation than merely to contemplate" (*Summa,* II-II, q. 188, a. 6). This incident also shows that while Thomas was greatly devoted to obedience, he did not hesitate to discuss this matter with the Pope in order to come to a mutual discernment. Thomas recognized his own gifts, and he must have known that the administration of a diocese was something he was not especially suited for. He also put his Dominican vocation first and foremost in his life, and did not allow anything else to interfere with that.

During these years in Italy, Thomas had greatly matured as a theologian and spiritual writer. When a critical need arose in Paris, his superiors asked him to return there to teach. This assignment came from the master general of the Order, John of Vercelli, and Thomas obeyed swiftly. However, this second stint of teaching as a master of theology in Paris would prove to be more difficult than his first one had been. The anti-mendicant controversy was boiling over again.

. . . .

Chapter Six

Return to Paris Amid
More Controversy

Thomas traveled with a small group of friars from Italy to Paris in the late summer of 1268, this time sailing part of the way instead of walking. They traveled along the coast of Italy to southern France, and from there sailed up the Rhone River. Some of his early biographers tell of a bad storm that swept upon them as they were going up the river. Thomas had a lifelong fear of storms, which may have stemmed from the tragic death of his baby sister during a storm when he was a toddler. As was his custom, he took out the relic of Saint Agnes that he always kept with him and prayed for her intercession. The skies soon cleared and they continued on their way, arriving in Paris in time for the new academic year beginning September 14. Stories like this show us a very human Thomas, who experienced fears and distress like all of us do.

A crisis had erupted in Paris that greatly concerned Thomas' superiors. It's likely that they asked Thomas to return so that he could help in dealing with it. Three things in particular had happened: first, the anti-mendicant controversy had been stirred up again; second, a backlash against the use of Aristotle in teaching the faith had developed; and third, some professors had taken Aristotle's ideas too far and in a way that at times contradicted Catholic teachings.

We can look at these briefly so as to understand better what Thomas had to deal with in Paris.

The Anti-mendicant Controversy

Around 1266 Gerard d'Abbeville, a friend of the infamous William of Saint-Amour, wrote a book attacking the mendicants. Essentially it repeated the same old charges, but it was enough to kindle more controversy. Naturally this caused problems for the Dominicans. Thomas used every means at his disposal to defend his beloved Order, including his disputations, sermons, and writings.

During this time, Thomas finished the second part of the *Summa Theologiae,* and toward the end of it he dealt with questions about the various states in life, including religious life. Some of the questions he asked might strike us as being odd, such as "Whether it is lawful for religious to wear coarser clothes than others?" (II-II, q. 187, a. 6). In other articles of this question he also asked if it is lawful for religious to beg and live on alms, or to teach and preach. He asked these questions (and answered "yes" to all of them) because the mendicants were being attacked on precisely these points. Knowing the historical context of his writing helps us to understand these questions of the *Summa,* which otherwise might seem strange. In the next question of that part, Thomas also asked, "Whether a religious order can be established for preaching or hearing confessions?" (II-II, q. 188, a. 4). That issue goes to the heart of the charism of the Dominicans— the Order of Preachers—so we can understand why Thomas defended it so vigorously. Thankfully the critics did not prevail, and the Dominicans and Franciscans have flourished ever since.

The Backlash Against the Use of Aristotle

This controversy is much more complex. Basically, it concerns a debate about how far Christian philosophers should go in adopting the ideas of Aristotle. Thomas had been a pioneering genius in using a form of Aristotelianism that could develop a philosophy in support of Christian faith. Others, however, opposed this because they were suspicious of the ideas of Aristotle, who knew nothing of the Christian faith. Sometimes this debate has been cast as an argument between followers of Aristotle on the one hand, and followers of Augustine on the other. But that is too simplistic an explanation, for Thomas was also very devoted to Augustine and drew much from him.[1] In addition, the so-called Augustinians used elements of Aristotelian thought. In any case, heated debates took place as the controversy swirled. Thomas, of course, had long been committed to drawing on aspects of Aristotle's thought. For Thomas, Aristotle was The Philosopher. But Thomas never used his ideas slavishly; instead, Thomas further developed ideas he found in Aristotle's

writings. Even amid this controversy Thomas remained committed to the proper use of Aristotle as an aid to the Christian faith.

The Other Extreme

On the other hand, some professors of the arts faculty in
Paris were going overboard in their use of Aristotle. Although
Aristotle's work on logic had been known in the West for a long
time, his other works were not. But from around the mid-
twelfth century, these works found their way to Europe via the
Arabic world. Some Arabic philosophers, notably Avicenna
and Averroes, had translated his works into their language and
wrote commentaries on them. By way of Spain, these books
started to become known in Europe through Latin translations.
However, some ideas found in both Aristotle and his commen-
tators were at odds with the Christian faith, such as the denial
of the idea of a personal God.

The biggest problem arose with an idea about the intellect,
drawn from a certain interpretation of Averroes: that there is
only one universal mind for all human beings. This, along with
some other ideas, came to be known as Latin Averroism (although
today this term is no longer used).[2] In the arts faculty, a professor
named Siger of Brabant was one of its biggest proponents.
Thomas was also drawn into this debate, since he always strove to
find what was true in everything. His short work on *The Unity of
the Intellect Against the Averroists,* written in 1270, refutes their
error. Thomas explains that there is not one universal mind for
the whole human race, but each person has his or her own intellect, for the intellect is a faculty of the human soul.

In all these controversies, Thomas used his mind and all his talents to defend what was most dear to him: the Catholic faith and his Dominican vocation. While Thomas was very open to using the ideas of Aristotle when they were useful, he applied his critical thinking skills in sorting things out. Above all, he prayed for the light of the Holy Spirit to guide his thinking and his teaching.

Thomas at Work

Thomas was called on to meet those three challenges in addition to his ordinary work of teaching, disputing, and preaching. During these years in Paris, Thomas also produced so many works that it can only be called phenomenal. Besides all the time he spent praying, his days were filled with teaching, dictating, and writing. While Thomas did write some things in his own hand, most of the time he dictated to his secretaries. Although it may seem unbelievable, it is well verified that he was capable of dictating to two or three secretaries at the same time. We have some testimonies to this, as stated by Friar Reginald and another secretary named Evan Garnit.[3] We don't know the names of Thomas' other secretaries.

In Paris, Thomas completed the second part of the *Summa Theologiae;* produced scriptural commentaries on the Gospels of Matthew and John, along with most of the letters of Saint Paul; wrote about a dozen commentaries on Aristotle; produced more disputed questions, such as the questions on evil, the virtues, the incarnation, in addition to seven series of quodlibetical questions; and wrote a series of at least fourteen shorter works.[4]

This is an incredible output. In order to do this, Thomas had the help of his secretaries in a sort of literary workshop where he could instruct them on which texts to copy, etc., and then he could build on that.[5] Being a teacher, Thomas also spent many hours in the classroom and in the hall of disputations. But above all, he was a friar, so he also spent many hours in prayer. He did all this without computers or electronic devices. And he traveled often, mostly on foot. Thomas was one of the most incredibly productive persons who ever lived.

As mentioned earlier, though Thomas doesn't speak of himself, he says something interesting in the *Summa* about how to cultivate a good memory. We can surmise from this that he himself used the four methods he outlines to remember something. These hints into the personal life of Thomas are precious for us:

1. Associate the thing with an unusual image, for we are more apt to remember visual images.

2. Use some sort of device to associate one thing with the next in order to recall a series of things.

3. Take some trouble to impress a certain thing on the mind so that it's not easily forgotten.

4. Finally, "we should often reflect on the things we wish to remember." Bringing them to mind often will reinforce them.[6]

Despite his genius, we shouldn't think that everything came easily to Thomas. He certainly had to make efforts to study, reflect, and remember. When he came to a difficult Scripture passage, he would often fast and pray in an effort to understand it. A story from his early biographers impresses this point.

Thomas was working on his commentary on the book of Isaiah. As he often did, he labored late into the night. One night Reginald was in his room and he could hear voices coming from Thomas' nearby room. One of them sounded like Thomas, but Reginald didn't recognize the two other voices.

The conversation went on for a long time. Suddenly, Thomas called out as he rushed to find his secretary. Despite the late hour, he asked Reginald to take dictation. Mystified, Reginald did as Thomas asked. Thomas' face was flushed and he spoke rapidly. After dictating for about an hour, he finally finished. As Reginald got up to leave, his curiosity overcame him. He asked what had so excited Thomas at that late hour.

After warning Reginald not to tell anyone as long as Thomas was alive, he confided that he had been praying and fasting for a long time, asking the Lord to help him understand the meaning of a certain passage in the book of Isaiah. Thomas said that the apostles Peter and Paul had appeared to him to teach him the meaning of the passage. Naturally, Reginald was dumbfounded. He only revealed these events after Thomas had died, and as part of his testimony about the great saint.

The Mission of Thomas

In the intense activity in Paris, Thomas worked incredibly hard because he was a man on a mission. Just as he intended the *Summa Theologiae* as a way of helping beginning students in theology, he produced his commentaries on Aristotle for the benefit of the young students in the arts faculty. The writings of Aristotle were growing in popularity, but because of the errors and misinterpretations that had arisen, some students were being misled even to a loss of their Catholic faith. Thomas took great pains to show that, understood correctly, Aristotle's ideas need not undermine faith but could strengthen it. Yes, in some areas the philosopher had erred, and Thomas pointed those out. He always sought a middle course between those who would completely reject Aristotle and those who would follow him into error. For Thomas, it was a matter of pastoral necessity. He saw his work not just as an intellectual exercise, but also as a mission for the good of the flock.

> The plight of young masters who had to teach Aristotle in the schools and who were always subject to being led astray into heresy, especially by Averroes, could not have been ignored. For this reason Thomas considered it his duty to young men in arts to supply them with commentaries that would be true to Aristotle, even when the latter's teaching had to be rejected, and free from error in philosophy. I am convinced that Thomas felt this apostolate to be urgent upon him, and one that he could minister to.[7]

Thomas was in full vigor, at the height of his powers. His writings also reflect some of his own personal and intellectual development and growth. Certainly we would expect to see this, for he was growing in holiness as well as in wisdom and learning. During this second regency, "there was an unusual development in his mentality, some profound, personal, psychic experience that affected his writing."[8] Instead of an overly intellectual approach, Thomas was developing a more comprehensive, even warmer viewpoint that showed his growth in mind and heart.

This change can be seen, for example, between the first and second parts of the *Summa*. Some of this could be accounted for by the subject matter, since the first part is more heavily philosophical. But that doesn't seem to be the whole explanation. For example, in his discussion of sorrow in the second part, Thomas speaks of how it can be alleviated by doing something enjoyable, having a good cry, talking to friends, contemplating the truth, taking a hot bath, and getting a good night's sleep. Like a good psychologist he says, "A hurtful thing hurts even more if we keep it shut up ... but if it is allowed to escape ... the inward sorrow is lessened. That is why when people burdened with sorrow make an outward show of their sorrow by tears or groans or even by words, their sorrow is lessened" (I-II, q. 38, a. 2). And in article five he quotes Augustine's citation of Ambrose: "Sleep restores the tired limbs to labor, refreshes the weary mind, and banishes sorrow." So the next time you need a good cry or a good sleep, you have the blessing of the Angelic Doctor, whom Saint John Paul II also called the *Doctor Humanitatis,* or Doctor of Humanity.

Chapter Seven

Teaching in Naples

After teaching in Paris for almost four years, Thomas was recalled to Italy. The Dominican master general, John of Vercelli, asked him to come back to help with the needs of the Roman province. We can imagine that Thomas would have been happy to leave the battles of Paris behind. A faculty strike was going on at the university, though it may not have affected the professors of theology. Thomas was still able to hold his *quodlibets* during Lent of 1272. Still, it seemed that some sort of controversy was always brewing in the university.

Despite that, Thomas was beloved to both his students and other professors. Some of the other masters, including the rector, wrote to the Dominicans pleading that they allow Thomas to stay in Paris. But it didn't work. The Roman province held its chapter in Florence that year and entrusted to Thomas a very special task: to open a new *studium generale* of theology. Thomas was free to choose its location. Not surprisingly, he chose Naples.

That location made good sense for several reasons. The king, Charles I, also known as Charles of Anjou, had consolidated his kingdom and Naples was at peace. It also had a vibrant atmosphere conducive to academic inquiry and studies. Charles I valued the Dominicans' contribution and was a patron of sorts. He even ordered that Thomas would be paid one ounce of gold each month for his teaching. This indicates that Thomas was not just teaching in the Dominican priory but in the university that Frederick II had founded earlier. Charles undoubtedly wanted Naples to be a center of learning that would attract students from all over Europe.

Naples was not very far from where Thomas grew up; it's less than forty miles from Monte Cassino. Thomas had family in the area, and while traveling he stopped to see his sister Theodora and her husband, Roger of San Severino. Thomas also went to visit his former student and friend, Cardinal Annibaldo d'Annibaldi (not to be confused with this cardinal's uncle, Cardinal Richard d'Annibaldo). But when Thomas arrived at his friend's castle in Molara, he found out that the cardinal had died just a few months earlier. This saddened Thomas, who had dedicated the second part of the *Catena Aurea* to his friend. To make matters worse, both Thomas and Reginald got sick with a fever. Thomas recovered fairly quickly, but Reginald got so sick that his life was in danger. Thomas applied his relic of Saint Agnes to Reginald and fervently prayed for his recovery. Thankfully, the fever broke and

Reginald got better. In gratitude, Thomas decided to hold a special dinner every year on the saint's feast day (January 21), but he was only able to do that once before he himself died.

After they were fully recovered, Thomas and his band traveled on to Naples, possibly visiting some of Thomas' relatives on the way. They probably arrived in Naples in early September, on time for the new school year. One of the Dominican students Thomas taught there was William of Tocco. Years later, after Thomas had died, William wrote a biography of Thomas that is recognized as one of the most reliable of the early sources.

In Naples, Thomas taught in the Dominican priory. His classes, however, were not restricted to Dominican students. They were university lectures, and students from the University of Naples could also attend them. Thomas lectured on the letters of Saint Paul as well as the Psalms. His commentary on Romans is one of the most beautiful and theologically rich of his works. Since it began his work on Saint Paul, Thomas started by commenting on Acts 9:15: "But the Lord said to him, [Ananias] 'Go, for he is an instrument whom I have chosen to bring my name before Gentiles and kings and before the people of Israel.'" The Latin text Thomas was using called Paul a "vessel of election" (*vas electionis*), so Thomas commented at length on this metaphor as applied to Paul. He says Paul was a golden vessel on account of his wisdom, a solid vessel because of his love. Paul was sent to carry the name of Christ to the nations, and Thomas reflects on this in a most beautiful way:

> But the vessel about which we are now speaking was filled with a precious liquid, the name of Christ, of which it is said: *your name is oil poured out* (Song 1:3). Hence, *to carry my*

name, for he seems to have been thoroughly filled with this
name: *I will write my name upon him* (Rev 3:12).[1]

As shown in this brief passage, Thomas often quotes other
texts of Scripture in commenting on the book he is studying.
While this method is different from that of modern Scripture
scholars, it shows the unity of the Bible and how the text often
holds different layers of meaning.

Medieval writers distinguished four senses of Scripture: the
literal, the allegorical, the moral, and the anagogical. Although
earlier writers had used these senses, medieval exegetes greatly
developed this method of interpretation.

1. *The literal sense,* for Thomas, meant what the author
    intended. He understood this sense in a way that was a
    development from previous authors. They had looked at
    this sense, generally, as being about what happened. In
    this they were not so interested in historical details but
    in the meaning of the events that were narrated. Thomas,
    however, moved beyond this to focus on the intention of
    the author. Simply speaking, that was what he meant by
    the literal sense. So in his view, if the author intended a
    spiritual meaning, that would be part of the literal sense.
    For example, when John narrates the account of the
    Samaritan woman at the well, he is not really interested
    in the mere details of Jesus meeting a woman and asking
    for a drink. He was interested in how Jesus brought this
    woman to faith. So Thomas would include that as part
    of the literal sense.

2. *The allegorical sense*: this had to do with seeing the events of the Old Testament as a type or indication of the events of the life of Christ and the mystery of the Church. The medieval masters saw this as a way of strengthening Christian faith, reading the Old Testament in the light of the New.

3. *The moral sense* (also called tropological): this concerned the lessons Scripture teaches on how we are to lead our lives, by practicing virtue and avoiding sin.

4. *The anagogical sense*: this concerned the ultimate goal that Scripture is intended to lead us to—eternal life. For example, texts that speak of Jerusalem as a glorified city were explained as pointing to heaven.

Thomas always considered the literal sense to be foundational, the one from which the other senses derived. In reading his scriptural commentaries, one is struck by his amazing knowledge of the text of the Bible. He quoted liberally from it, shedding light on one part of Scripture by using another. It leaves the reader with an incredible sense of the unity of the Bible. Thomas demonstrated beautifully that despite the differences between the various books, the Bible taken as a whole is God's gift to us, his word spoken to give us light.

Third Part of the Summa Theologiae

After returning to Italy in 1272, along with all his other tasks of teaching and writing, Thomas was hard at work on the third part of the *Summa*. In some ways this part of his great work is the easiest to read because it is about the life of Jesus. In it, Thomas follows the scriptural texts very closely and, in explaining them, uses an abundance of beautiful quotations from patristic sources. Those who are not familiar with the *Summa,* but would like to start reading it, would do well to start with this part. It is like spiritual reading based on the Gospel, taking into account the doctrinal aspects of the incarnation and what the Church teaches about Jesus.

From there, Thomas discusses the sacraments in general, and the sacraments of Baptism, Confirmation, and the Eucharist in particular. He began writing about the sacrament of Penance, but died before he could complete that part.

The third part of the *Summa* is especially fruitful for spiritual reading. For example, consider article 1 of question 79, where Thomas asks: Does the sacrament of the Eucharist bestow grace on the person who receives it? The answer of course is yes, but the four reasons for this that Thomas provides are truly beautiful as well as theologically profound.

The first reason is that this sacrament contains Christ himself, ". . . just as by coming into the world, he visibly bestowed the life of grace upon the world, according to John 1:17: 'Grace and truth came by Jesus Christ,' so also, by coming sacramentally into a person causes the life of grace, according to John 6:58: 'He who eats me, shall also live by me.'" In previous questions Thomas had explained how Jesus is the source of grace for us, how he received grace not just for himself but for all his members, and how Jesus communicates this grace through the sacraments. Among all the sacraments, the Eucharist is out-standing because it contains the very Body and Blood of Jesus himself.

The second reason we receive grace through the Eucharist is that it represents the passion of Christ, and so, Thomas says, "this sacrament works in the recipient the effect that Christ's passion wrought in the world." Stop for a moment and think about that: the passion of Christ sufficed for the redemption of the whole world, and we receive all its effects by receiving the Holy Eucharist. Imagine being present on Calvary as Jesus was dying on the cross. The Mass makes that spiritual reality present to us here and now. Thomas goes on: "Hence, Chrysostom says on the words, 'Immediately there came out blood and water' (Jn 19:34): 'Since the sacred mysteries derive their origin from thence, when you draw near to the awe-inspiring chalice, approach as if you were going to drink from Christ's own side.'"

The third reason this sacrament gives grace can be seen from the form it is given in: bread and wine. Just as food nourishes our body, this sacrament nourishes our soul: "This sacrament does for the spiritual life all that material food does for the bodily life, namely, by sustaining, giving increase, restoring, and giving delight. Accordingly, Ambrose says (*On the Sacraments,* v): 'This is the bread of everlasting life, which supports the substance of our soul.' And Chrysostom says (*Hom. xlvi on John*): 'When we desire it, he lets us feel him, and eat him, and embrace him.'"[2] Finally, this sacrament builds up the whole Church by joining us in a close union of love, just as the bread and wine are formed into a unity from many grains of wheat and many grapes pressed together. Quoting Augustine, Thomas writes: "Hence Augustine says (*Tract. xxvi on John*): 'Our Lord betokened his Body and Blood in things which out of many units are made into some one whole: for out of many grains is one thing made,' namely, bread; 'and many grapes flow into one thing,' namely, wine. And therefore he observes elsewhere (*Tract. xxvi on John*): 'O sacrament of piety, O sign of unity, O bond of charity!'"

The reflections and quotations that Thomas gives us can be used for meditation and prayer, especially while preparing for Mass and during Eucharistic adoration. His goal as a Dominican theologian was not only to form the mind, but also to share the fruits of prayer so that others would profit from it too.

Thomas and His Family

With all his work in teaching and writing, Thomas still found time to help his family. In August 1272, his sister Adelasia's husband, Roger of Aquila, died. In his will, he had appointed Thomas the executor of the estate, and Thomas took this role seriously. He carried it out with exactness and justice, and even visited King Charles I over some matters that came up regarding a relative to supervise the children's upbringing. It may seem unusual to think of Thomas handling financial transactions, but he willingly did whatever he could when called upon in such matters.

It seems that he kept fairly close ties with his brothers and sisters as much as he could. Now that he was back on his native soil, he had more opportunities to visit them, though he always gave priority to his duties as a Dominican friar. But the fact that he did maintain family ties to the extent that he could helps us to see Thomas as a well-balanced person who cared about his relationships with others.

Thomas and His Famous Abstraction

Some of the stories about Thomas make him seem like an absent-minded professor. His mind was so keen that he would often get lost in thought even when he was around other people. One such story comes from his time in Paris. In 1269, King Louis IX had invited Thomas to a banquet. Seated near the king, Thomas was completely quiet, his mind wrapped up in his thoughts. Suddenly he banged the table with his fist and shouted, "That settles the Manichees!" Then he called out, "Reginald, get up and write!" Everyone around was startled, but the king realized that Thomas had hit upon an important theological idea, so he sent for a scribe to take down what Thomas wanted to say. Later, realizing what he had done, Thomas apologized to the king, saying, "I thought I was at my study, where I had begun to think about the [Manichean] heresy."[3] Apparently this was not unusual. Reginald and others would often have to pull on his cape to bring him back to the present.

Besides his usual pensiveness, Thomas also fell into mystical states of prayer. Although Thomas didn't write about it himself, he had a reputation for holiness and profound prayer. The other friars would notice this about him, and sometimes it even happened in public. For example, on March 26, 1273, which was Passion Sunday, while Thomas was celebrating a public Mass, he fell deep into a mystical ecstasy, which expressed itself in the gift of tears. This went on for such a long time that one of the friars had to go up and shake him so that he could continue the Mass. Friar Reginald said he would often see Thomas this way.

CHAPTER EIGHT

• • • • • • • • • • • •

Last Days and Death

Thomas kept the same busy schedule he had followed for many years. He would rise early, celebrate Mass, and then devote more time to prayer. After that he would write and teach, pausing only for the midday meal. On December 6, 1273—the feast of Saint Nicholas—something happened that drastically changed Thomas' life. It is probably not a coincidence that it happened that day, since he had had a life-long devotion to Saint Nicholas. He was a popular saint in the Middle Ages, and in Paris Thomas had given a famous sermon about him.[1]

That morning, Thomas got up as he always did and went to celebrate Mass in the priory's chapel, which was also named after Saint Nicholas. As usual, Reginald served at the altar. Thomas prayed intensely and took his time. This day, however, as Thomas stood still at the altar for a long time, it looked like he had fallen into a trance. With his eyes closed, he seemed deep in prayer.

After waiting quite a while, Reginald got up, gently touched Thomas' arm, and asked if anything was wrong. But Thomas didn't seem to notice him. Reginald decided to wait. After what seemed like an extraordinarily long time, Thomas started the prayers again and finished the Mass.

As he left the chapel, Reginald approached and asked Thomas if they would continue working on the *Summa* at the usual time. But Thomas was not his usual self. He even seemed a bit dazed. Then he told Reginald he would not be giving any dictation that day. Reginald was shocked, for nothing before had ever kept Thomas from writing.

In the following days and weeks, Thomas did not return to writing his *Summa*—or anything else. Although he participated in community prayers, he seemed different somehow. Many of the friars noticed this and wondered what had happened to him.

When some of them asked Reginald about it, he said that Thomas had been like that since the feast of Saint Nicholas when he had fallen into a mystical state during Mass. Reginald didn't know exactly what was going on, but he thought that perhaps God had spoken to him.

Reginald didn't give up trying to get Thomas to work more on the *Summa*. But Thomas simply told him, "Reginald, I cannot." When Reginald asked why, Thomas said, "Reginald, I cannot because all that I have written seems like straw to me." Reginald must have been dumbfounded at Thomas' reply. When he pressed him for more information, Thomas finally answered, "Promise me, by the living God Almighty and by your loyalty to our Order and by the love you bear me, that you will never reveal, as long as I live, what I shall tell you. All that

I have written seems to me like straw compared to what has now been revealed to me."[2]

Leaving the *Summa* unfinished, Thomas put away his writing instruments and books. Though he no longer needed a secretary, his friend Reginald stayed with him in case he could help Thomas in any way.

What happened to Thomas? It was probably a combination of an intense mystical experience along with some sort of physical breakdown. He had pushed himself relentlessly for years, toiling with incredible energy to fulfill all the apostolic demands made on him. His productivity in terms of teaching and writing was simply amazing, but it came at a cost. His body could only take so much.

Shortly after his mystical experience, he went to the home of his sister Theodora to rest for a few weeks. The trip to the castle of San Severino, where she lived with her husband, Roger, was difficult for Thomas. That he took time for a rest indicates all was not well with his health. Reginald accompanied him on the trip. While they were there, Theodora noticed how different Thomas was and asked Reginald about it. He told her that Thomas had been like that ever since the feast of Saint Nicholas. After resting there for a few weeks, Thomas and Reginald returned to Naples either at the end of December or early January 1274.

When they returned, Thomas found that Pope Gregory X had asked him to attend the Council of Lyons, to be held that May. The purpose of the council was to try and reunite with the Greeks. Some years earlier Thomas had written a treatise on the matters separating East and West, and the Pope asked him to bring it with him.

Despite his poor state of health, Thomas obediently set out for Lyons around the end of January with Reginald and some others. At one point while they were traveling, Thomas accidentally hit his head very hard against a low-lying branch. It's not clear if he was walking or riding a donkey, but the blow stunned him. Although he continued the trip, it may have caused a blood clot in his brain that contributed to the cause of his death.[3]

The small group continued the trip. A few days later an envoy came from Monte Cassino, the famous Benedictine monastery where Thomas had studied as a boy. Abbot Bernard had sent the envoy to ask Thomas to come to explain a difficult passage from the writings of Saint Gregory. Thomas declined to go there, probably because his physical condition was getting harder to bear. It was a long, steep, and treacherous climb up the mountain to get to the monastery. Instead, he dictated a few pages on the topic to Reginald who wrote it all down.

By now it was near the end of February. Thomas was getting more and more tired with each passing day. His body seemed to be breaking down. Even with the donkey, the journey was becoming very difficult for him. They were near the castle of Maenza, where his niece Francesca lived, and decided to go there to rest a while. Once they got there, however, Thomas continued to grow weaker. Realizing his condition, Thomas asked to be taken to a nearby Cistercian monastery at Fossanova. He reportedly said that if the Lord was coming for him, it would be best that he be found in a monastery, not a castle. The monks at the monastery gave Thomas a guest room and helped take care of all his needs.

On March 4, Thomas asked Reginald to hear his final confession. After that, Thomas received Viaticum. In the presence of all the monks, who had gathered to pray at his bedside, Thomas declared: "I have taught and written much on this most holy Body and on the other sacraments, according to my faith in Christ and in the holy Roman Church, to whose judgment I submit all my teaching."[4]

News spread that Thomas, the gentle friar and brilliant theologian, was dying. The bishop of the area came to see him, as well as many Dominicans nearby. The day after receiving his final Communion, Thomas received the Anointing of the Sick. On Wednesday, March 7, 1274, early in the morning, Thomas Aquinas went to meet the Lord. The funeral was held two days later. The bishop came, as did many Dominicans, along with a great number of the Aquinas family and friends. They all recognized how holy Thomas had been, and knew that he was one of the greatest teachers the Church had ever known.

Canonization and Controversy

Right away people began to ask Thomas to intercede for their needs, and some people reported various favors and cures they had received. It wasn't long before the process of canonization was begun. Many people gave testimonies about how holy Thomas was. Reginald, his faithful friend, said he could declare before God that Thomas was as innocent as a little child, and that he had never consented to any serious sin.[5] Thomas was canonized on July 18, 1323, by Pope John XXII. This Pope greatly esteemed Thomas and had even purchased a whole set of Thomas' writings for his own use. Originally, March 7 was set as the feast day of Saint Thomas Aquinas. But since it fell in Lent, which precluded a more solemn celebration, in 1969 it was moved to January 28. That was the date that his relics were transferred to the Dominican church in Toulouse, France.

Just as Thomas was involved in controversies during his life, that continued even after his death. In March 1277, the bishop of Paris, Stephen Tempier, issued a list of 219 propositions that he condemned as being against the Catholic faith. This was directed against certain things being taught at the University of Paris. While Thomas was not the direct target, a few of the propositions were ideas that he had taught. Even the Dominican archbishop of Canterbury, Robert Kilwardby, criticized Thomas and his teaching. While we need not get into all the details of this controversy, it's a good reminder that even the greatest minds in the Church have been criticized by others, often unfairly. In the end, Thomas was vindicated, and in 1325 a later bishop of Paris rescinded the condemnation.[6]

The influence of Thomas' thought continued to grow. On April 15, 1567, the Dominican Pope Pius V named Thomas a Doctor of the Church and declared that his teaching is important for the whole Church and for all time. Later, in 1879, Pope Leo XIII wrote an encyclical *Aeterni Patris,* subtitled, "On the Restoration of Christian Philosophy in Catholic Schools in the Spirit of the Angelic Doctor, Saint Thomas Aquinas." With this document the Pope gave great impetus to a renewal of the study of Thomistic philosophy. This led to a resurgence of Thomism in the twentieth century, marked by great figures such as the Dominican Reginald Garrigou-Lagrange, Jacques Maritain, Etienne Gilson, and many others. After Vatican II there was a movement away from the writings and thought of Thomas, but he never completely faded. More recently, interest in Thomas' thought and writings has again increased. Pope John Paul II, in his encyclical *Fides et Ratio* (*On the Relationship of Faith and Reason*), emphasized the importance of Thomistic philosophy. The Pope wrote:

> Another of the great insights of Saint Thomas was his perception of the role of the Holy Spirit in the process by which knowledge matures into wisdom. From the first pages of his *Summa Theologiae* (see I, q. 1, a. 6), Aquinas was keen to show the primacy of the wisdom which is the gift of the Holy Spirit and which opens the way to a knowledge of divine realities. His theology allows us to understand what is distinctive of wisdom in its close link with faith and knowledge of the divine. This wisdom comes to know by way of connaturality; it presupposes faith and eventually formulates its right judgment on the basis of the truth of faith itself: "The wisdom named among the gifts of the Holy Spirit is distinct from the wisdom found among the intellectual virtues. This second wisdom is acquired through study, but the first 'comes from on high,' as Saint James puts it. This also distinguishes it from faith, since faith accepts divine truth as it is. But the gift of wisdom enables judgment according to divine truth" (see II-II, q. 45, a. 1, reply 2, and q. 45, a. 2).

I hope that after having read this brief biography of Thomas, you will be inspired to read something of his own writings. The next chapter will point out a few highlights of his spiritual teaching.

CHAPTER NINE

The Spiritual Legacy of Saint Thomas Aquinas

Countless books have been written about Thomas' spiritual legacy, and certainly this book can't duplicate it all. Here I would simply like to point out a few important ideas that can be drawn from his writings, ideas that can help us on our way to God from the heart of this great saint, who was on fire with God's love.

1. Virtue is about what is good, more than about what is difficult.

That might sound a little startling at first, but consider that some sinful things, like robbing a bank, are difficult to pull off. The difficulty doesn't make them virtuous. Only good acts are virtuous. With this idea, Thomas is merely emphasizing what

Saint Paul wrote: "And now faith, hope, and love abide, these three; and the greatest of these is love" (1 Cor 13:13). Ultimately, virtue is about love, the greatest good in our lives. Other things are measured according to that standard. Medieval people loved to see the world in terms of various hierarchies of ordered things. So in discussing the various virtues, Thomas constantly asks, "Is this virtue the greatest?" It's not an idle exercise, because in doing this he gets to the heart of what each virtue is about.

When he discusses the virtue of courage or fortitude, one of the cardinal virtues, Thomas asks if fortitude is the greatest virtue. One of the objections, which claims that fortitude is the greatest, runs thus: "Virtue is about that which is difficult and good. But fortitude is about most difficult things. Therefore it is the greatest of the virtues." In replying to this, Thomas says: "Virtue essentially regards the *good* rather than the *difficult*. Hence the greatness of a virtue is measured according to its *goodness* rather than its *difficulty*" (*Summa Theol.*, II-II, q. 123, a. 12, objection 2 and its reply, emphasis added).

That principle is so important and can save us from an unbalanced approach to the spiritual life. If we think that the most difficult things we can do are the most virtuous, then to be holy we would all have to be like Olympian athletes. The holiest person would be the one who could fast the most, get by on the least amount of sleep, walk around barefoot, or spend endless hours in church. But it doesn't work like that. The holiest person is the one who loves the most. Thomas' approach is incredibly liberating. It's probably also why he's not one of those saints known for extraordinary feats of asceticism. He became holy by doing the ordinary things in his life with an extraordinary amount of love. Of course, Thomas does not deny that we have to do difficult things and go against our inclinations in order to be holy. That's why fortitude is an important virtue. But the highest virtue is love. It's a matter of balance, of getting our priorities straight.

2. The mysteries of Christ are sources of grace for us.

In the third part of the *Summa Theologiae,* in which Thomas discusses the mystery of Jesus Christ, the great theologian speaks over and over about how Jesus is the source of grace. This teaching is rooted in the reality of who Jesus is: the Son of God made man; he is one divine Person with two natures, human and divine. But Thomas develops this in a unique way that has some very important implications for our spiritual life. He speaks about the humanity of Christ as an instrument of his divine nature, which produces in us grace and its spiritual effects.

Again, this is not a totally new idea since the Gospels themselves indicate this. For example, consider the woman with the hemorrhage who was determined simply to touch Jesus in order to be healed. The dense crowed was pressing on Jesus from every side, but that woman was the only one who touched Jesus with faith. When she did, power went out from him and immediately healed her (see Lk 8:43–48). As Thomas sees it, Jesus' divine power works through his humanity. Christ won our salvation especially through his death and resurrection. God is the source of salvation, and since Jesus is God, his sufferings on the cross work for our salvation. Jesus did this through his human nature, united to his divinity. And because the resurrected Jesus acts on our behalf from heaven, that power is still available to us today.

But how do we access that power? Thomas says there are two ways, through a contact by faith and through the sacraments: "Christ's passion, although corporeal, has yet a spiritual effect from the Godhead united: and therefore it secures its efficacy by spiritual contact—namely, by faith and the sacraments of faith, as the Apostle says (Rom 3:25): 'Whom God hath proposed to be a propitiation, through faith in his blood'" (*Summa Theol.,* q. 48, a. 6, obj. 2).

So what does this mean for us today? Whenever we read and meditate on the Gospel, by faith we are coming in contact with the mysteries of Christ, mysteries that are alive in him and have the power to make us holy. Every time we turn to Christ in faith, whether it is during formal prayer or at some moment of the day when we send up a spontaneous prayer, we are connecting to the spiritual powerhouse that Jesus is, the source of all our grace. And when we are living in God's grace, Jesus dwells within our soul. Power goes out from him to help us in whatever our needs are, just like power went out from him to heal the woman with the hemorrhage. The graces that he has in store for us are limitless. The only limit is our lack of faith.

Though we needn't get into the technical details, we can just note here that the ideas Thomas develops in this regard are based on what he calls "instrumental causality." In other words, certain effects are caused by some instrument or power that gets its power from something else. Here, the humanity of Jesus gets its power from his divinity, united in the personal union of his divine and human natures. Then Thomas takes this a step further and speaks about the sacraments. The sacraments are not only signs of grace but also instrumental causes, which can also bring about effects of grace. But they don't operate on their own; they have all their power from the grace of Christ. Along with faith, the sacraments are the most powerful ways that we can come into contact with the saving grace of Jesus Christ.

Here is a practical example of how this important teaching can help us receive the sacraments with greater faith and spiritual profit. Earlier we looked at the reasons why the sacrament of the Eucharist bestows grace on us. In addition, Thomas speaks of other spiritual effects of this sacrament: it leads us to eternal life, forgives venial sins, preserves us from future sins, benefits those we pray for, and leads us to a high degree of faith, hope, and love. He quotes Saint John Damascene, who says, "The fire of that desire within us, which is kindled by the burning coal [that is, the sacrament], will consume our sins and enlighten our hearts, so that we shall be inflamed and made like God" (*Summa Theol.*, III, q. 79, a. 8). If we could really grasp all these benefits, we would approach this sacrament with so much faith and confidence in Jesus that it would work miracles of grace in our lives.

The two areas mentioned are only like taking a dip in the great ocean of Thomas' writings. There are many areas where he offers fruitful themes for meditation and reflection. These include his beautiful comments on the virtues, the gift of grace, the gifts of the Holy Spirit, and so much more.

· · · · · · · · · · · ·

Prayer in Honor of
Saint Thomas Aquinas

Saint Thomas Aquinas, patron of students and Catholic schools, I thank God for the gifts of light and wisdom he bestowed on you, which you used to build up the Church in love. I thank God, too, for the wealth and richness of theological teaching you left us in your writings. You were a great teacher and also lived a holy life, seeking the Lord in all that you did. Pray for me that I might grow in faith, hope, and love, and be filled with the gifts of the Holy Spirit. I want to understand the word of God and put it into practice. Through your intercession may the truth of the Gospel spread throughout the whole world. Amen.

Reflection Questions

1. When Thomas was a toddler his infant sister was struck and killed by lightning when they were both napping in the same room. This traumatic experience may have been why Thomas seems to have had a lifelong fear of storms. Does this make him seem more human to you? If you have any fears or concerns that may be rooted in a difficult childhood experience, how do you cope with those? Would you think of Thomas as a good intercessor for your needs?

2. Thomas showed great determination in following his vocation to become a Dominican friar despite his family's fierce opposition. What does that say to you about the importance of being open to God's call in our lives? How might Thomas' example of courage under stress help those who are facing similar difficulties?

3. Despite the trouble he had with his family, Thomas always remained close to them and later helped them out in various ways. How can his example help those who are dealing with difficult family relationships?

4. Throughout his life, Thomas always sought the truth and to use his mind as a way to God. We live in an age of relativism, when many people do not accept the idea that we can even know truth at all. Yet Jesus said of himself, "I am the way, the truth, and the life" (Jn 14:6). How can you get to know Jesus better? How can Thomas help us to evangelize others by leading them to Jesus, who is Truth?

5. In posing questions in the *Summa Theologiae,* Thomas considers objections to the position he will take. Sometimes he even states the objections in a more compelling way than their proponents might have done. In our time, public discourse has often become uncivil, with less willingness to consider other points of view. What can Thomas teach us about how to have a civil discussion with someone who might disagree with our views?

6. What do you think Thomas meant when, near the end of his life, he said that all he had written seemed like straw in comparison to what he had seen? What does this tell us about the importance of our prayer life?

· · · · · · · · · · · ·

How to Read an Article of the *Summa*

This is the basic structure of an article:

1. Question—Thomas asks a question

2. Objections—Thomas lists the main objections to the position he will take. Most articles have about three objections, but some have more and a few have less.

3. "On the other hand" or the *sed contra*—Thomas makes a statement taking a position that differs from that stated in the objections. This usually represents the position Thomas himself will take, but not always. Thomas will sometimes clarify his own position in relation to the *sed contra*.

4. Response—Thomas gives his answer to the question. He will often distinguish various aspects for a more complete response, instead of simply saying "yes" or "no."

5. Replies to the objections—Thomas answers each of the objections.

Others may do it differently, but in reading an article I've found it most helpful to read the question, try to come up with my own answer, and then read the response Thomas gives. I always read it twice, sometimes three times, and then I go back to the objections. Again I try to come up with an answer to each objection, and then read Thomas' response. This is a fun and challenging way to read an article of the *Summa*. Some may prefer to go through each objection before reading the response, but Thomas often brings up points in the response that help to answer the objections.

The Virtue of Prudence: An Example of How the Summa *Can Help Us in Daily Life*

Sometimes people think of Thomas as an intellectual genius detached from the real world and they may wonder, "How can he help me?" They have a point in that it can be confusing to try to pick up the *Summa* and start reading. Some background is needed, and good books are available that can guide people through it (see the list on page 115). Yet many things that Thomas says are not only profound and spiritually moving, but also practical ideas that can help us live virtuously. A wonderful example of this is found in his treatment of the virtue of prudence, which helps us to made good decisions.

Certainly the saint most associated with discernment is Saint Ignatius of Loyola. His teachings are like the gold standard on that topic and are often used by people in making important life decisions. But what about the more concrete things we have to decide about each day? Most of these do not call for the well-developed process of Ignatian discernment, which calls for considerable spiritual energies. Once I was discussing this with another sister in my community, and she said, "Sometimes we just have to decide!"

When such decisions come up in our daily lives, Thomas offers us a way to make a good decision. He breaks down the virtue of prudence into three aspects and offers some tips on how to make a good decision in relation to these three things. I'll use a simple example, but the process can apply to any type of decision. Suppose Lent is coming up and I ask myself, "What can I do this Lent to become a better Christian?" The three steps that Thomas presents can help (see *Summa Theol.,* II-II, q. 47, a. 8, and q. 49).

1. The first step is to *take counsel*, to inquire into something so as to make a discovery. This might seem obvious because I already know what Lent is. But I could read something about it to come to a better understanding. I can recall that the Church recommends three general practices in Lent: prayer, fasting, and almsgiving. Which one do I want to focus on now? In taking counsel, I can do two things:

···· Look into myself and figure things out. What did I do during past Lents? How did those things work out? I might remember that last Lent I had resolved to give up watching TV, but then a friend invited me to watch a favorite show, so I did. What can I learn from that in order to make a more effective resolution?

···· I can also use information I've received from others. Maybe a family member told me I've been talking too much and don't listen. Can I take that as some good feedback instead of dismissing it?

2. The second step is *make a judgment,* that is, to actually decide what to do. After getting the data I need, I can evaluate what I learned in step one, and decide what I will do to grow spiritually during Lent. Maybe I'll resolve to listen more to others instead of talking so much. Or maybe I'll donate some time to volunteer for a good cause or to set aside a certain time for prayer. In making these decisions, Thomas suggests that we make a *well-reasoned* decision. He means to use foresight to anticipate any difficulties that might arise and take steps to avoid them. He also reminds us to pay attention to particular circumstances. For example, although fasting is good, I might have a health issue that means I shouldn't fast. The general types of penance need to be applied to my concrete situation. Thomas also says we should be cautious and not take foolish risks. Don't be reckless—so I shouldn't decide to do marathons of

prayer or fasting that I'll never maintain. But so far with all of this we're still in the realm of thought, not action. That's good, but I'll never do anything unless I can reach the next step.

3.   The third act is the most important one of all: Thomas calls it the act of executive command. In other words, we give ourselves a command to do something. That's the most important part of prudence, because it's not meant to be merely an intellectual exercise. It's meant to push us toward acting. Often we know what we should do to make our lives better, but we just don't want to do it and keep avoiding the issue. Sometimes we can make resolution after resolution, but never follow through. Why? It's because we haven't reached the moment of truth, when the virtue of prudence kicks in with its act of executive command and we start to do something positive. It's when we stop kidding ourselves. To get a sense of this, think about a time in your own life when you actually made a positive change. Maybe you had been thinking for a while that you should start eating in a more healthful way, but it was just an idea. Then a day came when you decided: "I'm going to *do* this, not just think about it anymore!" It was then that you got off the couch, put down the chips and the bowl of ice cream, and started to plan healthy meals. Or it could have been some other change. Whatever the needed change, this was the moment you stopped just thinking about something you wanted to do and actually *did* it. That's what the virtue

of prudence can do for us. By following the simple steps that Thomas outlines, we can make better decisions and be more open to grace in our lives.

Some Possible Plans for Reading the Summa Theologiae

Sometimes people think that Thomas' works are too hard to read. True, he does have his own style and some of the concepts are unfamiliar without philosophical training, but it would be a pity if we neglected his works simply because they are a bit challenging. Keep in mind also that some parts are easier to read because they are based more on Scripture and valuable ideas that are appealing and helpful. And recall that Thomas intended it as a work for beginners. Though we might think that those "beginners" must have really been quite advanced, in reality the *Summa* is not as hard to read as we might imagine. In some parts of it, Thomas does draw on philosophical concepts that lie behind his work. But Scholastic philosophy has been called a "common sense" philosophy since it is reality-based. Here are some possible plans for dipping into the *Summa* and reaping the great spiritual benefits we can find there. (See resources on page 115 for various editions of the *Summa,* both online and print.)

Plan 1. Read Parts of the *Summa* for Spiritual Reading

This is the easiest plan and probably the most spiritually beneficial. It is simply to read those parts of the *Summa* that have a direct impact on our spiritual life and can encourage us to grow in virtue and love of our Lord Jesus Christ. This plan is very flexible and can be adjusted easily to the desires of the reader.

a) Happiness and Virtue

Thomas organizes his treatment of the moral life around the idea of happiness. For Thomas, morality is not a depressing list of "should nots" but a wonderful quest for happiness by being the best persons that we can be. The happy life is a virtuous life. This plan starts by reading question 2 of the first part of the second part: In what does human happiness consist? In eight articles, Thomas considers the things most people seek to be happy. But do they really make us happy? Wealth, honor, power, fame, pleasure—none of these can satisfy the human heart. Reading his reflections on these things can help us consider if our lives are going in the right direction. Then in question 3, article 8, Thomas points us to the only one who can make us happy: God.

Then skip to the second part of the second part, where Thomas considers individual virtues. Feel free to pick and choose what most interests you. He starts with the theological virtues of faith, hope, and charity, and then the cardinal virtues of prudence, justice, temperance, and courage. Thomas explores the gifts of the Holy Spirit in relation to the various virtues. Some highlights from this part:

What is faith?	q. 1 and 4
What is hope?	q. 17 and 18
What is love?	q. 23–25 and 27–30
What is prudence?	q. 47 and 48
What is justice?	q. 57 and 58
Devotion and prayer:	q. 82 and 83

What is courage?   q. 123
What is temperance?   q. 141, 146–147

Gifts of the Holy Spirit:

> Understanding   q. 8
> Knowledge   q. 9
> Holy fear of the Lord   q. 19
> Wisdom   q. 45
> Counsel   q. 52
> Piety   q. 121
> Courage   q. 139

Also see I-II, on:

> the gifts in general   q. 68
> the beatitudes   q. 69
> fruits of the Holy Spirit   q. 70

b) The Life of Christ

In the third part of the *Summa,* Thomas writes about the incarnation and the life and work of Jesus Christ. Parts of this section are very biblical and have rich reflections on the life of Jesus and his mother, Mary. This section of the *Summa* considers Mary (q. 27–30),[1] the childhood of Jesus (q. 31–37), and the life of Christ (q. 38–45).

c) The Holy Eucharist

Question 79 on the effects of Holy Communion gives us a very beautiful meditation on the spiritual benefits of this sacrament.

Questions 73 to 78 cover the Eucharistic presence. These are very important articles on Catholic teaching about the Eucharist. But be aware that Thomas uses some important philosophical concepts when he discusses transubstantiation.

Plan 2: Read the *Summa* in a More Systematic Way

If you would like to do this, keep in mind that it is a lot of material to cover. So a good suggestion would be to set a goal that is more related to the process than the end result. For example, it would be easier to set a goal to read one article of the *Summa* a day or perhaps to spend ten minutes reading it. It isn't necessary to read the whole thing in order to benefit from it. Spending just a few minutes with Thomas each day, or most days of the week, will help you make small but steady progress in understanding the rich teaching of such a great spiritual master.

If you choose to do this, I would suggest starting with the third part of the *Summa,* since it is more accessible to most people. It is less heavily philosophical than the first part and uses a lot of Scripture. Also, the topics will be more familiar to most Catholics since it deals with Jesus and the sacraments.

Chronology

c. 1224/1225—Birth of Thomas at Roccasecca, Italy.

c. 1230–1239—Studies at Monte Cassino, Benedictine oblate.

1239–1244—Studies at Naples.

April 1244—Enters the Dominican Order at Naples.

1244–1245—Forced to stay at family castle in Roccasecca.

Autumn 1245—Allowed to leave and rejoin the Dominicans.

1245–1248—Studies in Paris under tutelage of Albert the Great.

1248–1252—Studies in Cologne with Albert the Great.

1250/51—Ordained to the priesthood in Cologne.

1252–1256—Bachelor of the *Sentences* in Paris.

Spring 1256—Becomes a master of theology in Paris.

1256–1259—Teaches theology in Paris; involved in anti-mendicant controversy; begins writing *Summa Contra Gentiles* (c. 1259).

1259—returns to Italy and goes to Naples; continues writing *Summa Contra Gentiles.*

1259–1261—Teaching in Naples.

1261–1265—Lector at Orvieto; completes *Summa Contra Gentiles.*

1264—Writes Office and hymns for the feast of *Corpus Christi.*

1265–1268—Teaching in Rome; begins *Summa Theologiae* (finishes *Prima Pars*).

Fall 1268—Returns to Paris for second period of teaching.

1268–1272—Second regency in Paris; completes *Secunda Pars* and begins *Tertia Pars.*

1272–1273 (December)—Returns to Naples to teach.

December 6, 1273—Mystical experience at Mass on feast of Saint Nicholas; stops writing.

March 7, 1274—Dies while en route to the Council of Lyons.

July 18, 1323—Canonized by Pope John XXII.

January 28, 1369—Relics transferred to Toulouse, France.

April 15, 1567—Declared a Doctor of the Church by Pope Pius V.

· · · · · · · · · · · ·

Selected Bibliography and Sources

A vast literature exists on Saint Thomas and his writings. The following selection focuses on books that are more accessible for those who would like an introduction to his life and work.

The biographies by James Weisheipl, OP, and Jean-Pierre Torrell, OP, are the most recent and up-to-date scholarly works. Where there was a difference in dates, I followed those given by Torrell since he uses more recent research about Saint Thomas.

The Writings of Saint Thomas Aquinas

A thorough online bibliography of Saint Thomas' works can be found at: http://www.home.duq.edu/~bonin/thomasbibliography.html.

Many works of Saint Thomas can be found in Latin and English at: http://dhspriory.org/thomas/.

De Sales University has an online Aquinas Translation Project of various texts: http://hosted.desales.edu/w4/philtheo/loughlin/ATP/.

Aquinas, Saint Thomas. *Albert and Thomas, Selected Writings.* Translated, edited, and introduced by Simon Tugwell, OP. Mahwah, NJ: Paulist Press, 1988.

———. *Aquinas's Shorter Summa.* Translated by Cyril Vollert, SJ. Manchester, NH: Sophia Institute Press, 2002.

———. *Selected Writings.* Edited and with an introduction and notes by Ralph McInerny New York: Penguin Books, 1998.

———. *Summa Contra Gentiles Books One through Four.* Translated and with an introduction and notes by Anton C. Pegis. Notre Dame, IN: University of Notre Dame Press, 1975.

———. *The Summa Theologica.* Literally translated by Fathers of the English Dominican Province. Second and revised edition. London: Burns Oates and Washbourne, 1920. Reissued, New York: Benziger Brothers, 1947.

Books about Saint Thomas and His Thought

Barron, Robert. *Thomas Aquinas: Spiritual Master.* New York: Crossroad, 2008.

Chesterton, G. K. *St. Thomas Aquinas.* New York: Sheed and Ward, 1933.

Bauerschmidt, Frederick Christian. *Thomas Aquinas: Faith, Reason, and Following Christ.* Oxford, England: Oxford University Press, 2015.

Chenu, Marie-Dominique, OP. *Aquinas and His Role in Theology.* Translated by Paul Philibert, OP. Collegeville, MN: Liturgical Press, 2002.

Davies, Brian. *Thomas Aquinas'* Summa Contra Gentiles*: A Guide and Commentary.* New York: Oxford University Press, 2016.

Davies, Brian. *Thomas Aquinas'* Summa Theologiae*: A Guide and Commentary.* New York: Oxford University Press, 2014.

Feser, Edward. *Aquinas (A Beginner's Guide).* Oxford, England: Oneworld Publications, 2009.

Kerr, Fergus. *Thomas Aquinas: A Very Short Introduction.* New York: Oxford University Press, 2009.

Kreeft, Peter. *Practical Theology: Spiritual Direction from St. Thomas Aquinas.* San Francisco: Ignatius Press, 2014.

———. *A Summa of the* Summa. San Francisco: Ignatius Press, 1990.

———. *A Shorter* Summa. San Francisco: Ignatius Press, 1993.

McInerny, Ralph M. *St. Thomas Aquinas.* Notre Dame: University of Notre Dame Press, 1982.

Murray, Paul, OP. *Aquinas at Prayer: The Bible, Mysticism, and Poetry.* London: Bloomsbury Publishing, 2013.

Nichols, Aidan. *Discovering Aquinas: An Introduction to His Life, Work, and Influence.* Grand Rapids, MI: Eerdmans Publishing, 2003.

O'Donnell, Robert. *Hooked on Philosophy: Aquinas Made Easy.* New York: Alba House, 1995.

Pieper, Josef. *Guide to Thomas Aquinas.* San Francisco: Ignatius Press, 1991.

Schwartz, Daniel. *Aquinas on Friendship.* New York: Oxford University Press, 2007.

Selman, Francis. *Aquinas 101: A Basic Introduction to the Thought of St. Thomas Aquinas.* Notre Dame, IN: Christian Classics, 2007.

Torrell, Jean-Pierre, OP. *Saint Thomas Aquinas.* vol. 1, *The Person and His Work.* Washington, DC: The Catholic University of America Press, 1996.

Torrell, Jean-Pierre, OP. *Saint Thomas Aquinas.* vol. 2, *Spiritual Master.* Washington, DC: The Catholic University of America Press, 2003.

Turner, Denys. *Thomas Aquinas: A Portrait.* New Haven: Yale University Press, 2014.

Weisheipl, James A., OP. *Friar Thomas D'Aquino: His Life, Thought, and Work.* Garden City, NY: Doubleday & Company, Inc., 1974.

Notes

INTRODUCTION

1. See Christopher Shields and Robert Pasnau, *The Philosophy of Aquinas* (New York: Oxford University Press, 2016), 1.

2. See Thomas Aquinas, *Summa Theologiae,* II-II, q. 23, a 1. Also see Daniel Schwartz, *Aquinas on Friendship* (New York: Oxford University Press, 2007).

3. See James A. Weisheipl, OP, *Friar Thomas D'Aquino: His Life, Thought, and Work* (New York: Doubleday and Company, 1974).

CHAPTER ONE

1. See Jean-Pierre Torrell, OP, *Saint Thomas Aquinas: The Person and His Work,* vol. 1 (Washington, DC: Catholic University of America Press, 1996), 4.

2. See Boniface Ramsey, *John Cassian: The Conferences* (Mahwah, NJ: Paulist Press, 1997), 5–7.

3. Torrell, *Saint Thomas Aquinas*, 7.

4. Charism in this context is a gift from the Holy Spirit given to the founder of a religious institute. The charism involves a distinctive spirituality and gift for mission in the Church.

5. Weisheipl concludes it probably did happen, though the historical sources are not well-founded on this point, *Friar Thomas,* p. 30–31; Torrell mentions this only briefly, *Saint Thomas Aquinas,* p. 9.

6. Note: A group today known as the Angelic Warfare Confraternity promotes this devotion: http://www.angelicwarfareconfraternity.org/history/.

7. Torrell, *Saint Thomas Aquinas,* 11.

8. Ibid., n. 83, p. 17.

9. *Summa Theologiae,* II-II, q. 101, a. 4, quoting Saint Jerome, epistle to Heliodorus, 2.

CHAPTER TWO

1. Torrell, *Saint Thomas Aquinas,* 280.

2. See Martin Tracey, "The Moral Thought of Albert the Great," in *A Companion to Albert the Great*, ed. Irven Resnick (Boston: Brill, 2013).

3. See Weisheipl, *Friar Thomas D'Aquino,* 44–45.

4. *Summa Theologiae,* II-II, q. 161, a. 6.

CHAPTER THREE

1. See Torrell, *Saint Thomas Aquinas,* 41.

2. Ibid., 38–39.

3. Weisheipl, *Friar Thomas D'Aquino,* 76. Torrell, *Saint Thomas Aquinas,* 45–47, discusses the likelihood that Thomas also lectured on

the *Sentences* later while in Rome 1265/66. He thinks it is likely, based on the work of some good scholars.

4. See Thomas Aquinas, *An Apology for the Religious Orders,* ed. Fr. John Procter, STM (London: Sands & Co., 1902).

5. Thomas Aquinas, *An Apology for the Religious Orders,* 373.

6. Weisheipl, *Friar Thomas D'Aquinas,* 90.

7. Torrell, *Saint Thomas Aquinas,* 51.

8. Psalm 103 in the Vulgate edition Thomas used.

9. Quote from letter of Pope Alexander IV dated June 7, 1256, as found in Weisheipl, *Friar Thomas D'Aquino,* 94.

10. The Aquinas Institute in Lander, WY, is currently working to publish translations of all the works of Thomas, including the Scripture commentaries.

11. From *Quodlibet* 4, 18, quoted on p. xxi in the Introduction to vol. 1 of the *Summa Theologiae,* edited by Thomas Gilby, OP (Cambridge: Cambridge University Press, 2006).

12. For sermons that Thomas preached at the university, see Thomas Aquinas, *The Academic Sermons* (Washington, DC: Catholic University of America Press, 2010).

13. See http://hosted.desales.edu/w4/philtheo/loughlin/ATP/Sermons/Pentecost_Sermon.html.

CHAPTER FOUR

1. Torrell, *Saint Thomas Aquinas,* 101–102.

2. *Summa Contra Gentiles,* bk I, ch. 2, quoting Saint Hilary of Poitiers, trans. Anton C. Pegis (South Bend, IN: University of Notre Dame Press, 1975).

3. See Torrell, *Saint Thomas Aquinas,* 129–132.

Chapter Five

1. Weisheipl, *Friar Thomas D'Aquinas*, 198.

2. See Torrell, *Saint Thomas Aquinas,* 161–62.

3. *Summa Theologiae,* I, q. 3, a. 8.

4. *Summa Theologiae,* Prologue (Notre Dame, IN: Christian Classics, 1981), xix.

5. Ibid.

6. See Weisheipl, *Friar Thomas D'Aquinas*, 214.

7. Ibid., 200.

Chapter Six

1. For more on this topic see *Aquinas the Augustinian*, ed. Michael Dauphinais, Barry David, and Matthew Levering (Washington, DC: Catholic University of America Press, 2007).

2. See Torrell, *Saint Thomas Aquinas,* 191–196.

3. See Weisheipl, *Friar Thomas D'Aquino*, 243.

4. For a catalog of Thomas' writings, many with links to English translations, see http://dhspriory.org/thomas/.

5. See Torrell, *Saint Thomas Aquinas,* 243.

6. *Summa Theologiae,* II-II, q. 49, a 1, ad 2.

7. Weisheipl, *Friar Thomas D'Aquino*, 280–281.

8. Ibid., 244.

Chapter Seven

1. Thomas Aquinas, *Commentary on the Letter of St. Paul to the Romans* (Lander, WY: Aquinas Institute, 2012), 2.

2. Excerpts about Aquinas' four reasons are taken from *Summa Theologiae*, III, q. 79, a. 1.

3. Weisheipl, *Friar Thomas D'Aquino*, 236.

CHAPTER EIGHT

1. Can be found at: http://www.stnicholascenter.org/pages/aquinas/.

2. Weisheipl, *Friar Thomas D'Aquino*, 322.

3. See Weisheipl, *Friar Thomas D'Aquino*, 329; he thinks that Thomas suffered a subdural hematoma.

4. Weisheipl, *Friar Thomas D'Aquino*, 326.

5. See Ibid., 329.

6. See Torrell, *Saint Thomas Aquinas,* 298–303, for more details on this controversy.

APPENDIX

1. If you read this section, keep in mind that the dogma of the Immaculate Conception was not fully developed in the Middle Ages, so we can ignore Thomas' opinion that Mary was conceived with original sin and later sanctified in the womb. The theological difficulty had to do with Mary's need for a redeemer: if she never had the stain of original sin, how could Christ be her Redeemer? The Franciscan theologian John Duns Scotus found the solution that Mary was redeemed in view of Christ's merits, which in her case preserved her from original sin.

BOOKS & MEDIA

A mission of the Daughters of St. Paul

As apostles of Jesus Christ, evangelizing today's world:

We are CALLED to holiness
by God's living Word and Eucharist.

We COMMUNICATE the Gospel message
through our lives and through all
available forms of media.

We SERVE the Church
by responding to the hopes and needs
of all people with the Word of God,
in the spirit of St. Paul.

For more information visit our website:
www.pauline.org.

BOOKS & MEDIA

The Daughters of St. Paul operate book and media centers at the following addresses. Visit, call, or write the one nearest you today, or find us at www.paulinestore.org.

CALIFORNIA

3908 Sepulveda Blvd, Culver City, CA 90230	310-397-8676
3250 Middlefield Road, Menlo Park, CA 94025	650-369-4230

FLORIDA

145 S.W. 107th Avenue, Miami, FL 33174	305-559-6715

HAWAII

1143 Bishop Street, Honolulu, HI 96813	808-521-2731

ILLINOIS

172 North Michigan Avenue, Chicago, IL 60601	312-346-4228

LOUISIANA

4403 Veterans Memorial Blvd, Metairie, LA 70006	504-887-7631

MASSACHUSETTS

885 Providence Hwy, Dedham, MA 02026	781-326-5385

MISSOURI

9804 Watson Road, St. Louis, MO 63126	314-965-3512

NEW YORK

115 E. 29th Street, New York City, NY 10016	212-754-1110

SOUTH CAROLINA

243 King Street, Charleston, SC 29401	843-577-0175

TEXAS

No book center; for parish exhibits or outreach evangelization, contact: 210-569-0500, or SanAntonio@paulinemedia.com, or P.O. Box 761416, San Antonio, TX 78245

VIRGINIA

1025 King Street, Alexandria, VA 22314	703-549-3806

CANADA

3022 Dufferin Street, Toronto, ON M6B 3T5	416-781-9131